White-tailed Deer Monitoring Protocol for the Heartland Network Inventory and Monitoring Program

Natural Resource Report NPS/HTLN/NRR—2007/014

David G. Peitz, J. Tyler Cribbs, Jennifer L. Haack, Gareth A. Rowell, Lloyd W. Morrison, and Mike D. DeBacker
National Park Service
Heartland I&M Network
Wilson's Creek National Battlefield
6424 West Farm Road 182
Republic, MO 65738

August 2007

U.S. Department of the Interior
National Park Service
Natural Resource Program Center
Fort Collins, Colorado

The Natural Resource Publication series addresses natural resource topics that are of interest and applicability to a broad readership in the National Park Service and to others in the management of natural resources, including the scientific community, the public, and the NPS conservation and environmental constituencies. Manuscripts are peer-reviewed to ensure that the information is scientifically credible, technically accurate, appropriately written for the intended audience, and is designed and published in a professional manner.

Natural Resource Reports are the designated medium for disseminating high priority, current natural resource management information with managerial application. The series targets a general, diverse audience, and may contain NPS policy considerations or address sensitive issues of management applicability. Examples of the diverse array of reports published in this series include vital signs monitoring plans; monitoring protocols; "how to" resource management papers; proceedings of resource management workshops or conferences; annual reports of resource programs or divisions of the Natural Resource Program Center; resource action plans; fact sheets; and regularly-published newsletters.

Views, statements, findings, conclusions, recommendations and data in this report are solely those of the author(s) and do not necessarily reflect views and policies of the U.S. Department of the Interior, NPS. Mention of trade names or commercial products does not constitute endorsement or recommendation for use by the National Park Service.

Printed copies of reports in these series may be produced in a limited quantity and they are only available as long as the supply lasts. This report is also available from the Heartland I&M Network website (http://www.nature.nps.gov/im/units/HTLN) on the internet, or by sending a request to the address on the back cover.

Please cite this publication as:

NPS D-70, August 2007

Acknowledgements

The National Park Service's Inventory and Monitoring Program provided funding for the development of this white-tailed deer monitoring protocol, and continue to fund monitoring of the resource in network parks. Numerous NPS personnel have contributed in-kind support to the development of this protocol, and continue to assist with annual surveys. We acknowledge important input from resource managers during a breakout session of the 2005 Heartland Network annual meeting to help refine the monitoring objectives. This protocol has benefited from comments by Dr Paul Lukacs on an earlier version. Peer review by Dr. Lynn Robbins, Dr. Jonathan Jenks, and Dr. David Leslie greatly improved the final protocol.

Contents

Contents

Contents

List of Figures

List of Tables

White-tailed Deer Monitoring Protocol for the Heartland Network Inventory and Monitoring Program

1.0 Background and Objectives

1.1 Issue Being Addressed and Rationale for Monitoring White-tailed Deer Populations

Since European settlement, white-tailed deer *(Odocoileus virginianus)* populations in North America have experienced enormous changes in size and distribution. Once abundant, deer numbers declined to near extinction by the early 1900s. Clearing of forested lands and unrestricted hunting contributed heavily to the decline of this species (Stoll and Donohoe 1973, Dennis 1983). Declines in deer numbers were especially prevalent in the East and Midwest sections of the country where much of the land was converted for row-crop farming.

Regulated white-tailed deer hunting and extermination of most of their natural predators has led to unprecedented population growth throughout their range. With natural deer habitat severely reduced, row-crop agriculture and other agriculture practices provide artificial food sources that deer utilize. The ability of white-tailed deer to adapt to human disturbance has also aided in the recovery of this species. Urban sprawl benefits deer by fragmenting continuous blocks of forested lands into small sections with increased edge habitat favored by deer and rarely available for hunting. Therefore, deer experience high rates of population growth as long as food is available in these small blocks of patchy habitat. Grass and forb production is greater in these areas, as is mast production by oaks, hickories, and other trees when compared to larger blocks of forested land (Peitz et al. 2001). Urban sprawl also redistributes deer by eliminating habitat in one area, thereby concentrating deer in available habitat in another (Shafer-Nolan 1997).

Deer become vulnerable to overpopulation, disease, and starvation in the absence of natural predators and hunting. When deer occur in high densities, diseases are transmitted more readily. In years when forage or mast production is restricted due to climatic conditions, starvation or poor herd health can occur. High deer populations also contribute to over-browsing of vegetation, which leads to plant mortality, decreased plant reproduction, and may favor less preferred exotic species (McShea and Rappole 1997). This shift in species assemblages can reduce plant diversity at a local level and cause changes in the functioning of prairie and woodland communities. Rare and sensitive plant species may be influenced negatively by deer foraging, although the influence of deer on the status of most rare and sensitive plant species is largely unknown. Many studies have shown that deer can have a negative effect on developing forestland (Crouch and Paulson 1968, Horsely and Marquis 1983, Marquis 1981). Browsing on young tree seedlings causes stunted growth as well as mortality (Michael 1992, Mladenoff and Stearns 1993). Research has shown that in some situations damage from deer, as well as mice and rabbits, may be a key impediment to forest restoration (Crouch and Paulson 1968, Strole and Anderson 1992).

White-tailed deer are often viewed as an important component of park ecosystems. Deer have a tremendous following among the public and many parks provide information on the status of deer through their interpretive programs. This information is generally anecdotal in nature, however. White-tailed deer can present a safety hazard to motorist and park visitors when populations are high. High deer numbers increase the number of vehicle-deer collisions and the resulting property damage and personal injuries. In some cases, vehicle-deer collisions can result in the loss of human life. Deer also disperse ticks that may carry Lyme disease (Connelly et al. 1987), a debilitating immune system illness transmitted to humans by the bite of ticks. Ticks carrying other diseases transmittable to humans, such as Rocky Mountain Spotted Fever and Ehrlichiosis, may be spread by deer as well. Information on the status and trends in deer population size helps park managers determine if control measures are necessary in order to protect other park resources and improve visitor safety.

Against a backdrop of urban sprawl, altered ecosystems, and concerns over visitor safety on National Park Service lands, we proposed monitoring white-tailed deer populations. Long-term trends in deer abundance provide one measure of assessing their potential as a problem for a park. Documenting long-term patterns in deer numbers allows one to evaluate correlations with changes in vegetation (e.g., through restoration of the cultural landscape). With this information resource managers can more effectively identify and potentially mitigate damage caused to vegetation communities and endangered plant populations by deer. Monitoring data also helps managers assess safety risks from collisions and disease transmission. Long-term monitoring of deer numbers is critical in evaluating any population control measures a park may implement.

1.2 Historical Development of White-Tailed Deer Monitoring in Network Parks

Monitoring trends in the composition and abundance of white-tailed deer populations is critical to understanding herd health over the long-term (Gee et al. 1994). The impacts of deer on vegetation, disease transmission, and vehicle-deer collisions can only be thoroughly assessed with a good knowledge of trends in population size. Monitoring deer populations may help protect ecosystem integrity, which is defined as the capability of an environment to support and maintain a balanced, integrated, adaptive community of organisms having a species composition, diversity, and functional organization comparable to that of natural habitat of the region (Karr and Dudley 1981). Information on deer population trends is vital when mitigating visitor health concerns and the incidents of vehicle-deer collisions.

Deer surveys have been conducted sporadically in several network parks. Homestead National Monument of America, Nebraska, for example, has used rushing surveys to assess deer numbers. While this method is effective in small parks, it is of little value on large acreages (>100 hectares). Cuyahoga Valley National Recreation Area, Ohio, has an ongoing monitoring program that has been in effect since 1988. Spotlight surveys taken from a train and along roadways located within the park are utilized to assess deer numbers. Spotlight counts have also been used by graduate students from the University of Arkansas-Monticello to assess deer numbers at Arkansas Post National Memorial, Arkansas. During 2003, Wilson's Creek National Battlefield staff assisted students from Missouri State University in surveying deer numbers as part of a class project. This protocol serves to formalize and standardize deer surveying techniques across the Heartland Network Inventory and Monitoring Program (HTLN).

During initial protocol development, "Distance" sampling techniques where examined. However, assumptions critical to the use of "Distance" sampling methods could not be met and this method of surveying deer was dropped. At an annual meeting of the HTLN in August 2005, many aspects of deer monitoring were discussed with natural resource managers from various network parks. Issues such as the impact of deer on vegetation, disease transmission, concern over vehicle-deer collisions in and around parks, and the impacts of deer on neighboring private lands were examined. In the end, resource managers felt tracking an index of deer numbers through time was the most efficient and sustainable use of resources. The impacts of deer on vegetation, disease transmission, and vehicle-deer collisions can only be thoroughly assessed with a good knowledge of trends in population size. Resource managers, using trend data, will secure funding to research and mitigate the impacts of deer as needed.

Measurable Objectives

1. Document annual changes in white-tailed deer numbers. **Justification:** *Significant annual changes in deer numbers may signal the presence of illegal deer harvest, disease, or other acute factors of concern for park management.*
2. Determine long-term trends in white-tailed deer numbers. **Justification:** *Understanding decadal trends in deer number will help park management determine if measures need to be taken to maintain herd health, minimize vegetation damage within a park, or alleviate visitor health concerns.*
3. Annually map locations of white-tailed deer observed. **Justification:** *Mapping deer locations allows park management to assess the influences of management actions on deer usage of an area, habitat type, etc.*

2.0 Sampling Design

2.1 Population being Monitored

The populations of interest are the white-tailed deer herds within each park. For safety reasons, sampling will be done along existing park roads rather than random transects. Because the habitat types encountered along park roads are not necessarily in proportion to the distribution of habitat types in the overall parks, and the location of park roads may affect the distribution of deer, resulting density estimates may not be representative of absolute densities within the overall park. Thus, our density estimates are considered to be an *index* of relative population density, which is positively correlated with absolute population density, but to an unknown degree.

Sampling is limited to winter months, before spring green up (January through mid March). The deer present at this time will be impacting herd size and park resources through the next year. In many situations, a knowledge of the buck:doe and fawn:doe ratios would be desirable. But most bucks will have shed their antlers by this time and fawns will be of sufficient size to be mistaken as older does. Therefore, buck:doe and fawn:doe ratios may not be calculated. Overall herd density is best estimated during winter months, however, as declines in deer numbers through fawn mortality and hunting around park lands have stabilized. It is more desirable to have an estimate of herd densities on National Park Service lands than having information on herd ratios.

If these same lands were to be hunted, then ratios would assume more importance and more intense sampling to estimate each would be justified.

Although it is not possible to determine the absolute number of deer in a park at any time from these methods, such information on relative abundance is of value in detecting trends. In a meeting regarding white-tailed deer monitoring held in 2005, resource managers from the representative parks indicated that determining absolute deer density in the parks was not a priority. Resource managers did desire information on changes in deer populations over time, so that if white-tailed deer ever became an important management issue, data would be available indicating population trends. More in-depth (and expensive) surveys aimed at estimating absolute abundances could then be implemented (see Supplemental Document #2).

2.2 Spatial Design

Sampling locations or 'routes' are selected as described in SOP #4, "Establishing Survey Routes". Maps showing the survey routes at Arkansas Post National Monument, Arkansas; Pea Ridge National Military Park, Arkansas; and Wilson's Creek National Battlefield, Missouri are given in Figures 1 – 3.

Tour Road

Park Boundary

0   70   140   280   420   560
Meters
Scale 1:8,000

N
W — E
S

Figure 1. White-tailed deer survey route at Arkansas Post National Memorial, Arkansas.

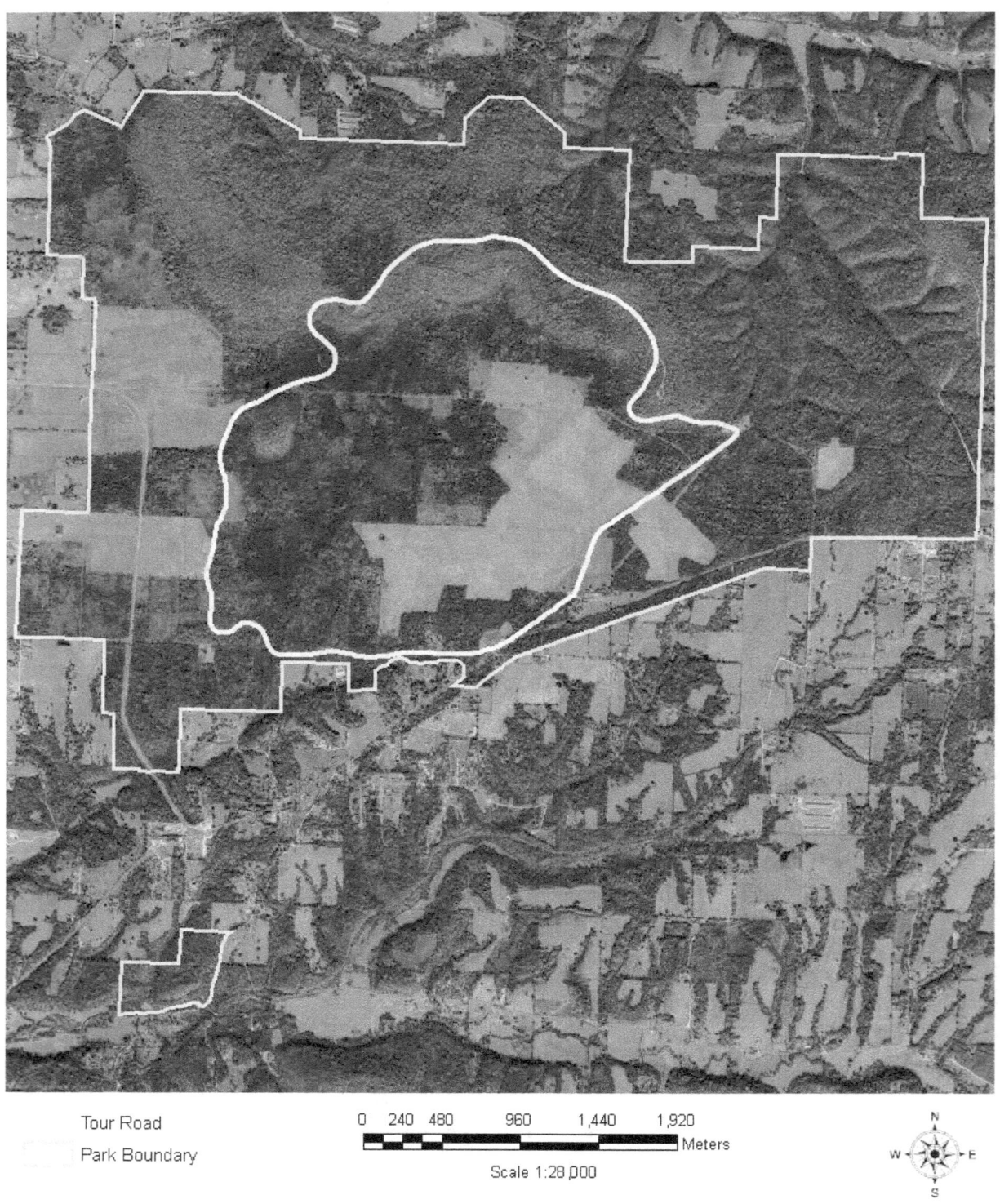

Tour Road

Park Boundary

0   240   480   960   1,440   1,920
                                                Meters
                Scale 1:28,000

Figure 2. White-tailed deer survey route at Pea Ridge National Military Park, Arkansas.

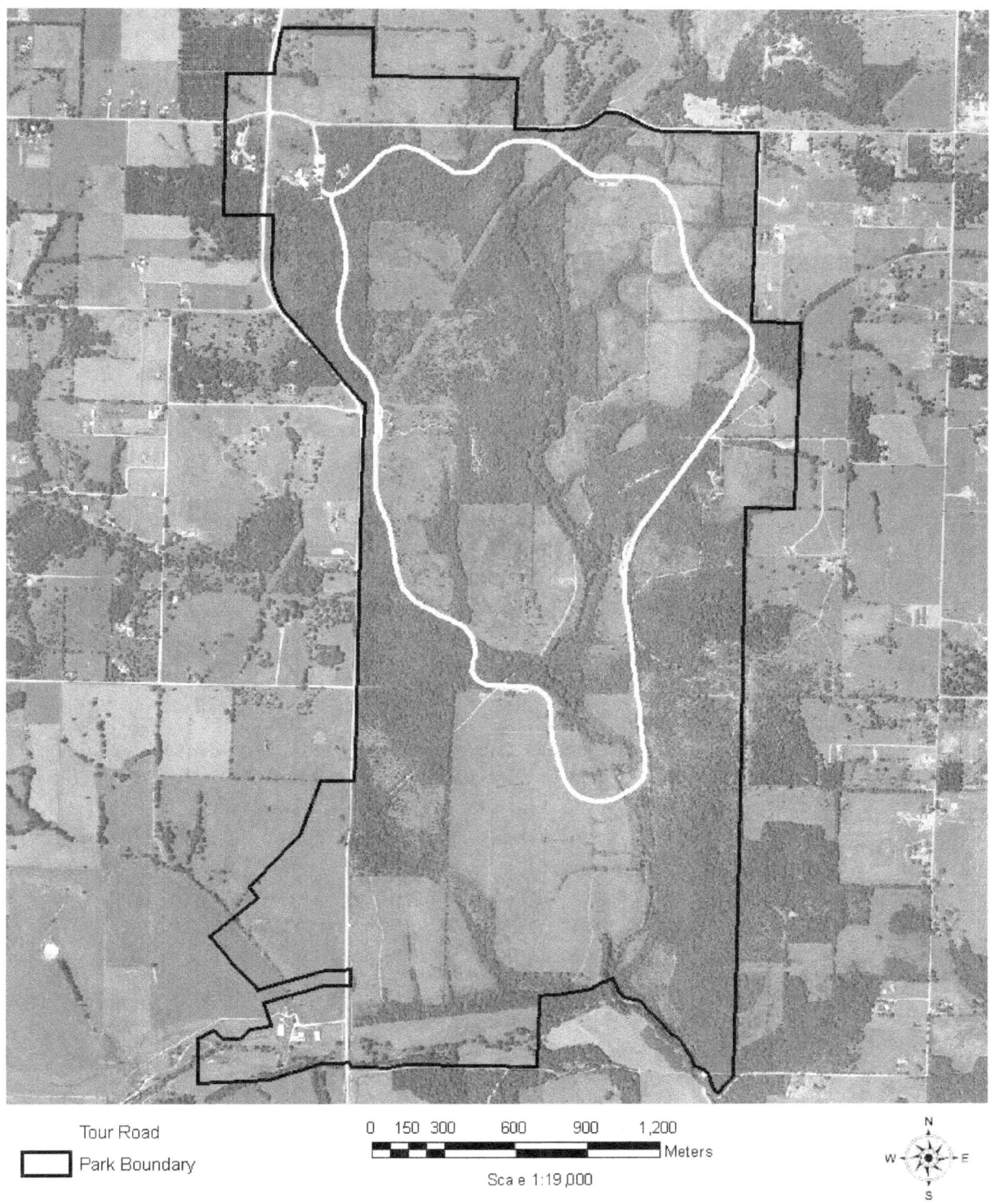

Tour Road
Park Boundary

0 150 300   600   900   1,200
Meters
Scale 1:19,000

N
W E
S

Figure 3. White-tailed deer survey route at Wilson's Creek National Battlefield, Missouri.

2.3 Revisit Design

All survey routes within each HTLN park unit monitored for white-tailed deer will be sampled annually. To obtain a measure of variability, a minimum of three density estimates from three different nights are needed. Ideally, six density estimates from six different nights will be obtained annually. The maximum count from three consecutive surveys conducted each night will be used as the density estimate for that date. Visibility assessments will be recorded on the first night a survey is conducted to get an annual estimate of the area over which deer can be seen. Changing vegetation in each HTLN park requires that visibility estimates be made each year and that the area sampled is not predetermined from aerial photos or maps. Visibility assessments begin as soon as the last spotlight survey is completed.

2.4 Response Design

Surveys commence one hour after official sunset and follow predetermined survey routes. An index of relative density is obtained by counting the number of deer observed with a spotlight along the monitoring route. Deer positions are recorded as distance and azimuth from the observation vehicle, and later converted to UTM coordinates using GIS. The observable area is defined by taking measurements perpendicular to the sample route out to a distance beyond which deer are not visible. This area is determined at 0.16 km (1/10th mile) intervals along the survey route, immediately following deer counts on the first survey day.

2.5 Rationale for Selecting this Sampling Design over Others

Dozens of different monitoring programs utilizing a multitude of sampling approaches are currently in place throughout North America to determine local white-tailed deer population densities. Most common survey methods allow for population estimates, but no single method will adequately sample the complete population. The spotlight survey is widely accepted as a practical method for estimating trends in the density of a deer population in an area. Sampling involves spotlighting deer at night to obtain some estimate of the number of deer present in an area and then determining the total area visible during the survey. Deer density is simply the number of deer observed divided by the area visible during the survey. In practice, the method documented in this protocol is basically a line transect estimate of deer numbers with the total area visible during a survey determined.

Aerial surveys, mark and recapture surveys, fecal pellet counts, the use of infrared triggered cameras, 'rushing', and distance sampling are different types of deer survey methods that have been considered for use in estimating population densities and size of white-tailed deer herds in HTLN parks. Camouflaging ground cover and limited visibility from the air inhibit accurate aerial surveys; furthermore aerial surveys are expensive to implement and require experienced observers to conduct (Bates 2004; Haroldson et al. 2003). Aerial surveys are difficult to arrange and generally require snow on the ground during a survey to aid in locating and seeing deer, especially if deer are visually sighted. Infrared imaging does not require visually spotting deer. However, skilled operators are required to effectively use the equipment and to differentiate between deer observations and those of other animals. Since HTLN parks are spread across the

Midwest Region, numerous contracts with different agencies would have to be made in order to carry out such surveys.

The accuracy of a mark and recapture survey is dependent upon the number of deer marked and the number of deer re-sighted. Kilpatrick et al. (1997) calculated that it takes a minimum of 4.4 hours to capture and mark each deer. If just 10% of a herd as small as 100 individuals were marked, it would require at least 44 hours or one week to capture and mark deer. Herd sizes in HTLN parks are much larger than 100 individuals; thus the field hours to capture enough deer would be cost-prohibitive. The number of surveys required to obtain an adequate number of re-sighted individuals for an accurate estimate of the population could be cost-prohibitive as well.

Fecal pellet counts along transect lines is a survey type that has been used for many years. These counts require many field hours to complete, however, and the cost associated with field hours required to complete a survey would be prohibitive. Another factor to consider with fecal pellet counts is that of logistics. A minimum of two multi-day trips would be required to each HTLN park unit to conduct a survey. The first trip is needed to clear areas of deer feces so an accurate time interval for pellet deposition can be determined. During the second trip, fecal pellet groups deposited since the first trip are counted. Fecal pellet counts are generally limiting with regards to the amount of area that can be covered because of the labor involved.

Remote cameras have been used to census white-tailed deer (Jacobson et al. 1997). This method is cost prohibitive as well. Initial camera cost and the annual cost for film development and camera replacements would limit the scope of our deer monitoring to only the smallest HTLN parks. One camera per 20 ha (48 acres) was recommended for the National Capital Region Network (Bates 2004), for example. Using infrared cameras also requires a considerable amount of time be devoted to processing pictures, identifying each deer, and determining accurate estimates of the population.

'Rushing' involves placing observers in hidden locations along a line on one end of a park. Another group starts on the opposite end of the park in an attempt to scare the deer so they run by the hidden observers who in turn count their numbers. This type of survey is not possible given the size of most HTLN park units. Also, it may not be the best way to acquire accurate numbers of the deer population as individuals can be counted multiple times by different observers.

The distance method of sampling takes into account decreasing detection probabilities as distance from an observer increases. Densities of the target organism are calculated based on the shape of an empirically determined detection function (Buckland et al. 2001). This method cannot be employed because several main assumptions are violated (e.g., placement of transects is not random, locations of transects [roads] affect the distribution of deer, etc.). See the critical comments of Dr. Paul Lukacs, an expert on distance sampling, in Supplemental Document #1 regarding this, and other sampling options.

3.0 Field Methods

3.1 Field Season Preparations, Field Schedule, and Equipment Setup

Prior to the field season each year, usually beginning the previous November or December, all observers should review this entire protocol, including all standard operating procedures (SOPs). Observers should pay special attention to the tasks described in SOP #1 "Before the Field Season" and SOP #2 "Training Observers". A review on estimating distance is particularly important each year to assure quality data is collected (see SOP #2). All of the equipment and supplies listed in SOP #1 should be organized and made ready for the field season; copies of the field data forms in Appendix A should be made. Twenty-five percent of all field data sheets should be copied to write-in-the-rain paper.

Staff workloads and unpredictable weather (e.g., the onset of extremely cold weather, periods of rain or snow, extreme icy conditions) necessitate maintaining some flexibility in scheduling the sequence and duration of sampling trips. Sampling dates should be scheduled and logistics organized prior to the start of each field season, however. Alternative sampling dates should be identified as well. Three replicated deer surveys should be scheduled for completion each field day at a park. Visibility estimates should be scheduled for the first day at a park, after deer surveys are complete. One field day at a park should be scheduled weekly starting the first of January. An effort should be made to complete six field days at a park, three being the minimum.

Influences of weather on deer activity and detectability need to be considered during counts. During periods of high wind, deer move from open to closed areas (Linsdale and Tomich 1953, Loveless 1964, Ozoga and Gysel 1972, Beier and McCullough 1990). Therefore, counts are restricted to periods without high winds (i.e., sustained winds >30 km/hr; 18.6 m/hr) to optimize seeing deer in open habitats with greater visibility. Although heavy rain does not influence deer activities (Zagata and Haugen 1974, Michael 1970, Beier and McCullough 1990), periods of heavy rain will influence visibility, and thus should be avoided. Likewise, snow fall greater than moderate will influence visibility, and thus should be avoided. Snow on the ground limits food availability, thus affecting patterns of deer movement as they seek out areas of higher food availability. Therefore, deer should not be surveyed during periods of significant snow accumulations as this will add unnecessary variability into count data across years. Weather criteria for conducting deer counts are outlined in SOP #1.

3.2 Sampling Methods

Permanent sampling routes, selected from existing all-weather roads within a park, are used to survey deer. Due to the nature and purpose of most parks, and for safety reasons, it is not recommended to drive off road to complete surveys. Once arriving at the park, park maps are used to familiarize each observer with the park, and determine the starting point, direction and sequence each section will be surveyed. A global positioning system (GPS) is used to mark the beginning and ending points along each survey route.

Each day the project manager splits the observation team into a pair of deer observers, a data recorder, and a driver. The data recorder is responsible for ensuring all data fields listed on the data dictionary of the GPS unit are filled in and the location of each deer or deer group is recorded. The data recorder also fills out a paper copy of all data observations. Deer observers are responsible for locating deer and accurately taking distance measures from the survey vehicle to the deer or deer group. Observers are also responsible for recording the angle of the deer or deer group from the survey vehicle. Along with the obvious chore of driving, the driver is responsible for measuring all weather parameters and assisting with data recording if needed. For safety reasons the driver should not be involved with recording data if the survey vehicle is moving.

Each member of the sampling team is responsible for keeping track of their equipment and/or data sheets. Before leaving the field each night, all equipment is accounted for and data sheets are checked for completeness and passed on to the project manager. The project manager is responsible for the safekeeping and organization of the data sheets and ensuring data entry. The data recorder is responsible for downloading all data from the GPS unit. At the end of each year's sampling, a trip report including weather conditions, logistical problems, any subsequent departure from the protocol, etc. should be written by the project manager.

3.3 Conducting the Spotlight Survey

Spotlight surveys will establish a relative index of white-tailed deer population density at each HTLN park unit. Methods for conducting the spotlight survey are given in SOP #5 "Conducting the Spotlight Survey" and are summarized here. Surveys are conducted from a survey vehicle moving no more then 16 km/hr (10 mi/hr) using two 1,000,000 candlepower spotlights. All deer seen along the survey route are counted and their location recorded using GPS technologies. Deer counts are made by two observers, one seated on the left and one on the right side of the vehicle. Distances from the stopped survey vehicle to all deer are determined with a rangefinder or, for deer < 20 m from the vehicle, by visual estimates. Deer are usually observed in groups, in which case distance is taken or estimated to the center-most deer in the group. In order to map locations of deer, the direction and angle of all deer or deer groups from the survey vehicle are recorded as well. From pilot data, it was observed that the highest number of deer counted each night generally occurred within the first couple of hours following official sunset (See Supplemental Document #4). However, on occasion the maximum number of deer counted occurred in the second or third replicate. Therefore, three surveys commencing one hour after official sunset will be used to count deer numbers each night. Jester and Dillard (2001) and Shult and Armstrong (1983) recommend starting surveys one hour after official sunset to maximize deer observed.

3.4 Establishing Visibility during Surveys

Determining the area surveyed for white-tailed deer is critical for obtaining an accurate estimate of deer density in the survey area. SOP #6 "Establishing Visibility during Surveys" gives a detailed description of how the area visible during surveys is determined; a brief summary is presented here. Visibility estimates are taken on the first night after the surveys are completed by recording the perpendicular distances from the survey vehicle to a point beyond which deer would not be visible. Visibility is monitored every 0.16 km (1/10th mile) along the survey route.

The location each perpendicular measure is taken is marked using GPS technologies. In an attempt to get a more robust picture of how much area is being surveyed along the route, the location of the survey vehicle should be adjusted slightly if objects are encountered that block the true area observed during a survey. For example, if the view of an open field is blocked by a single cedar tree in the ditch next to the survey vehicle, move the vehicle forward or backward to see the field. Using GIS technologies, perpendicular distances are plotted on a map, a polygon is created, and the survey area is determined.

4.0 Data Management

4.1 Overview of Database Design

The design of the deer monitoring database is centered on GPS locations. Each GPS location is associated with deer observed during spotlight surveys. Unlike most monitoring databases, location is the primary field in the database. Furthermore, locations of observations are not predetermined. In the Natural Resource Data Template, these locations are called "Data_Locations" rather than simply "Locations" (National Park Service, 2006). There is a one-to-one relationship between data locations and field data, in contrast to planned locations which have a one-to-many relationship with field data. Data locations are typically required in monitoring databases for linear transect surveys, where exact locations of target features are not known. In addition to GPS location data, the deer monitoring database includes a field table for deer observations. As previously mentioned, it is this table that corresponds one-to-one with the GPS data. This attribute table includes number of deer, distance from viewer, vegetation type (upland forest, upland scrub, grass/prairie), date and time of observation, GPS related information (Max_PDOP, Correction Type, Receiver Type, and other technical information), DeerID (unique integer) and EventID. The EventID field links the field data many-to-one to the SamplingEvents table. The SamplingEvents table contains weather and physical conditions including: moon illumination and beginning and ending values for temperature, humidity, wind, wind direction, and precipitation.

4.2 Metadata Procedures

National Park Service natural resource databases are required to include FGDC standard metadata. Wide distribution of metadata enables potential users to identify exactly what monitoring data is available. It also provides instructions regarding how to contact data stewards. Creation of metadata has been greatly facilitated by ESRI ArcGIS utilities that automatically generate spatial metadata. The ArcGIS utilities do not provide similar automation for attributes. Currently, these have to be entered by hand. Certain Access metadata generators are being developed "in-house" by WASO I&M developers. These are currently in beta form and have not been widely distributed. Once metadata has been created, it should be saved in XML format. It can be converted to text or html at a later date using the FGDC "mp" utility. Metadata is archived in the geodatabase and by WASO I&M. Currently the WASO copy is submitted using the NR-GIS metadata clearinghouse. XML format is required for WASO metadata. Metadata is archived with WASO with the submission of the monitoring protocol. It should be updated with each protocol revision.

4.3 Data Archival Procedures

Data archive is the most important part of data management activity. Servers go down and don't come back. The data manager needs to be able to restore data to alternate servers or workstations. In this sense, a reliable tape backup device is more critical than the server itself. For the deer database and other monitoring databases, we run complete backups (no incremental backups) each Monday, Wednesday, and Friday. Monday tapes are held for a month. Archive tapes are made quarterly and stored for 18 months. Back-up logs are reviewed on every job and file restores are run once per month just to be sure the system is working.

Like other monitoring databases, the white-tailed deer monitoring database is also secured by file archives stored on the server. The database is maintained under a directory called DeerSurveys under the production drive called "L". The database immediately below this directory is the production copy of the database. Under DeerSurveys is also a subdirectory called "dev" that is short for "development". All backups and earlier versions are stored under this directory.

5.0 Analysis and Reporting

A critical component of any long-term monitoring protocol is a consistent and systematic way of analyzing and reporting on information (data) collected. The information must serve two purposes: (1) describe the current condition or status of a deer population and (2) detect changes in a population through time. The variable selected for data summary purposes is an index of relative population density. This annual index of relative population density provides information to park managers on trends in park deer populations and may provide feedback on the effects of implemented management efforts (e.g., population control or vegetation restoration efforts). As additional data are collected, trend analysis using time-series analysis or repeated measures will be explored as tools to detect temporal trends in deer density data.

SOP #9 "Data Summary and Analysis" gives step-by-step details on how to: 1) determine annual deer population densities, 2) calculate annual density means and standard deviations and 3) determine percent annual change in deer densities. Deer population densities should be analyzed and compared against previous estimates every year surveys are completed.

5.1 Recommendations for Routine Data Summaries and Analyses

Population density, defined as the number of individuals/km^2 of sample area, provides an index with which annual change or long-term trends can be measured. To calculate this index, two pieces of information are needed: (1) the maximum number of individuals within the sample area and (2) the size of the area sampled. Daily maximum numbers of deer are obtained from count data collected each night during spotlight surveys. The size of the area sampled for deer is determined annually, during the first survey night, by measuring at 0.16 km (1/10th mile) intervals along the survey route the perpendicular distances from the survey vehicle to a point beyond which deer would not be visible. The point perpendicular distances are measured using GPS technologies. Using GIS technologies, perpendicular distances from the first survey nights are plotted on a map, a polygon is created, and the annual survey area determined (see SOP #9 "Data Summary and Analysis"). Annual survey areas, by definition, include all deer observations. An estimate of the average annual population density and standard deviation is determined from replicate maximum deer counts for that year. The range in population densities each year is determined from replicate maximum values as well. The percent change in annual deer densities within the survey area should be calculated and reported annually.

5.2 Recommendations for Long-term Trend Analyses

An underlying purpose of the HTLN is to design and implement long-term ecological monitoring to evaluate the integrity of park ecosystems and contribute to the understanding of ecosystem processes. The approach towards long-term analysis of monitoring data is therefore critical to meet this goal. HTLN is currently planning and implementing several techniques to address long-term data analysis for monitoring projects. The simplest, yet, perhaps, most important method of long-term monitoring data analysis is simply graphing data through time with an estimate of variability. Trend is easily inferred from a graphical presentation. Furthermore, the likelihood that an observed trend is significant can be determined from the range of the standard deviation, and its overlap among sample periods. Graphs are easily interpretable, and, as such, serve as useful tools for interpreting monitoring results to managers.

5.3 Recommendations for Reporting Results

To facilitate timely dissemination of monitoring results, annual status reports should be completed by September 1st of the year data is collected. More extensive summary reports, including trend analysis, should be completed every five to ten years depending on the rate of change in the deer community and the need for summary information to guide resource management. Summary reports may be used in place of annual reports for that year. All reports must follow National Park Service Natural Resource Technical Report formatting style. Refer to SOP #10 "Reporting" for details on report structure and style.

Tables and figures (including pictures) in a report should be placed within the text or immediately following the literature cited section. Tables and figures should be numbered in sequence regardless of where they are located. Table captions are placed at the top of a table, while figure captions are placed below the figure. Horizontal lines are used to separate the table caption from column headings, column headings from the table, and to signify the end of the table. Vertical lines should not be used in tables. Tables and figures should contain information not presented in the body of the text, thereby minimizing redundancy.

6.0 Personnel Requirements and Training

6.1 Roles and Responsibilities

The project manager is the lead ecologist for implementing this monitoring protocol, and is supervised by the Program Coordinator for HTLN. The data management aspect of the monitoring effort is the shared responsibility of the project manager, the GIS specialist, and the data manager. Typically, the project manager and GIS specialist are responsible for data collection. The project manager is responsible for data entry, data verification, and validation, as well as data summary, analysis, and reporting. The data manager is responsible for data archiving, data security, dissemination, and database design. The data manager, in collaboration with the project manager and GIS specialist, develops data entry forms and other database features as part of quality assurance, and automates report generation. The data manager is ultimately responsible that adequate QA/QC procedures are built into the database management system and appropriate data handling procedures are followed.

6.2 Qualifications and Training

The most essential component for the collection of credible, high-quality data is competent observers. Good night vision is critical. Many deer are seen at a distance and only visible because of the reflection of light from the tapetum lucidum in their eyes. As well as being able to visually identify deer, observers should be tested frequently on their ability to estimate distances or measure them using a laser rangefinder. Time should also be invested in training personnel to estimate the distance from themselves to deer within different habitats. This will require training in the field (see SOP #2, "Training Observers") to become proficient with the use of a laser rangefinder and to gain experience with estimating distances in different habitat types. The quality of the observer will determine the quality of the data.

7.0 Operational Requirements

7.1 Annual Workload and Field Schedule

White-tailed deer surveys will begin no sooner than the first week of January and end no later then the second full week of March, a period that coincides with peak visibility through brush and trees. Inclement weather and personnel workloads will preclude the scheduling of sampling events to specific annual dates. Deer surveys may be scheduled for the third week of March if winter storms are unusually late. Monitoring efforts will require a four person crew. Approximately six field days for each park are required to complete deer sampling. One additional day of travel should be planned for each field day at Arkansas Post National Memorial.

7.2 Facility and Equipment Needs

The nature of deer survey work does not require special facilities beyond normal office space and equipment storage needs. Table 1.01 list the field equipment needs for one crew. If two or more crews work simultaneously, equipment requirements will increase accordingly.

7.3 Startup Costs and Budget Considerations

Personnel expenses for field work are based on a crew of four people: an ecologist, a GIS specialist, and two subject to furlough biological science technicians. Six field days should be planned for both Wilson's Creek National Battlefield, Missouri, and Pea Ridge National Military Park, Arkansas, and 12 field days for Arkansas Post National Memorial, Arkansas. Field costs will vary from year to year depending on the skill level and size of the crew. Data management/reporting expenses include staff time of biological science technicians, a GIS specialist, project manager, and data manager. Startup costs include the purchase of equipment and supplies listed in Table 1.01 as well as maintenance or replacement of equipment shared among multiple projects (e.g. GPS units, cameras, vehicles).

Table 1. Startup and annual costs, for monitoring white-tailed deer populations in Heartland Network Inventory and Monitoring Program parks.

Category	Startup Cost	Annual Cost
Field work (salary)	7,150.00	14,750.00
Travel	2,140.00	3,400.00
Data management/reporting	11,490.00	11,490.00
Startup equipment costs	9,860.00	--
Annual equipment/supplies	--	1,500.00
Administrative support and overhead	7,660.00	5,570.00
TOTAL	38,300.00	36,710.00

7.4 Procedure for Revising the Protocol and Archiving Previous Versions

Over time, revisions to both the protocol narrative and to specific SOPs are to be expected. Careful documentation of changes to the protocol, and a library of previous protocol versions are essential for maintaining consistency in data collection and for appropriate treatment of the data during data summary and analysis. The MS Access database for each monitoring component contains a field that identifies which version of the protocol was being used when the data was collected. The rationale for dividing a sampling protocol into a protocol narrative with supporting SOPs is based on the following:

- The protocol narrative is a general overview of the protocol that gives the history and justification for doing the work and an overview of the sampling methods, but does not provide all of the methodological details. The protocol narrative will only be revised if major changes are made to the protocol.
- The SOPs, in contrast, are very specific step-by-step instructions for performing a given task. They are expected to be revised more frequently than the protocol narrative.
- When an SOP is revised, in most cases, it is not necessary to revise the protocol narrative to reflect the specific changes made to the SOP.
- All versions of the protocol narrative and SOPs will be archived in a protocol library.

The steps for changing the protocol (either the protocol narrative or the SOPs) are outlined in SOP #12, "Revising the Protocol". Each SOP contains a revision history log that should be filled out each time an SOP is revised to explain why the change was made and to assign a new version number to the revised SOP. The new version of the SOP or protocol narrative should then be archived in the HTLN protocol library under the appropriate folder.

8.0 References

Bates, S. 2004. White-tailed deer density monitoring protocol version 1.0: distance and pellet group surveys. National Capital Region Network Inventory and Monitoring Program, Washington, D.C., USA.

Beier P. and D.R. McCullough. 1990. Factors influencing white-tailed deer activity patterns and habitat use. Wildlife Monographs 109:1-51.

Buckland, S.T., D.R. Anderson, K.P. Burnham, J.L. Laake, D.L. Borchers and L. Thomas. 2001. Introduction to distance sampling: estimating abundance of biological populations. Oxford University Press Inc. New York, NY, USA.

Connelly, N. A., D. J. Decker and S. Wear. 1987. Public tolerance of deer in a suburban environment: implications for management and control. Eastern Wildlife Damage Control Conference 3:207-217.

Crouch, G.L. and N. R. Paulson. 1968. Effects of protection from deer on survival and growth of Douglas-fir seedlings. USDA Forest Service, Pacific Northwest Forest Range Experiment Station Reserve, Research Note 94.

Dennis, D. F. 1983. An analysis of Ohio's forest resources. USDA Forest Service, Northeast Research Station, Research Bulletin NE-75.

Gee, K.L., M.D. Porter, S. Demarais, F.C. Bryant and G. VanVreede. 1994. White-tailed deer: their foods and management in the cross timbers (second edition). The Samuel Roberts Noble Foundation, Inc. Ardmore, OK, USA.

Haroldson, B.S., E.P. Wiggers, J. Beringer, L.P. Hansen and J.B. McAninch. 2003. Evaluation of aerial thermal imaging for detecting white-tailed deer in a deciduous forest environment. Wildlife Society Bulletin 31:1188-1197.

Horsely, S.B. and D.A. Marquis. 1983. Interference by weeds and deer with Allegheny hardwood reproduction. Canadian Journal of Forest Research 13:61-69.

Jacobson, H.A. J.C. Kroll, R.W. Browning, B.H. Koerth and M.H. Conway. 1997. Infrared-triggered cameras for censusing white-tailed deer. Wildlife Society Bulletin 25:547-556.

Jester S. and J. Dillard. 2001. Conducting white-tailed deer spotlight surveys in the cross-timbers and prairie region of north and central Texas. http://www.tpwd.state.tx.us/publications/pwdpubs/media/pwd_rp_w7000_1126.pdf.

Karr, J.R. and D.R. Dudley. 1981. Ecological perspective on water quality goals. Environmental Management 5:55-68.

Kilpatrick, H.J., S.M. Spohr and A.J. DeNicola. 1997. Darting urban deer: techniques and technology. Wildlife Society Bulletin 25:542-546.

Lindsdale, J.M. and P.Q. Tomich. 1953. A herd of mule deer. University of California Press, Berkeley, CA, USA.

Loveless, C.M. 1964. Some relationships between wintering mule deer and the physical environment. Transactions of the North American Wildlife and Natural Resources Conference. 29:415-531.

Marquis, D.A. 1981. Effect of deer browsing on timber production in Allegheny hardwood forests of northwestern Pennsylvania. USDA Forest Service Research Paper NE-475.

McShea, W.J. and J.H. Rappole. 1997. The science and politics of managing deer within a protected area. Wildlife Society Bulletin 25:443-446.

Michael, E.D. 1970. Activity pattern of white-tailed deer in south Texas. Texas Journal of Science 21:417-438.

Michael, E.D. 1992. Impact of deer browsing on regeneration of balsam fir in Canaan Valley, West Virginia. Northeastern Journal of Applied Forestry 9:89-90.

Mladenoff, D.J. and F. Stearns. 1993. Eastern hemlock regeneration and deer browsing in the Northern Great Lakes region: a re-examination and model simulation. Conservation Biology 7:889-900.

National Park Service. 2006. Natural Resource Database Template Version 3.1 documentation. Natural Resource Program Center, Office of Inventory, Monitoring, and Evaluation, Fort Collins, CO, USA.

Ozoga, J.J. and L.W. Gysel. 1972. Response of white-tailed deer to winter weather. Journal of Wildlife Management 36:892-896.

Peitz, D.G., M.G. Shelton and P.A. Tappe. 2001. Forage production after thinning a natural loblolly pine-hardwood stand to different basal areas. Wildlife Society Bulletin 29:687-705.

Shafer-Nolan, A. L. 1997. The science and politics of deer overabundance at Cuyahoga Valley National Recreation Area, Ohio. Wildlife Society Bulletin 25:457-461.

Shult, M.J. and B. Armstrong. 1983. Deer census techniques. http://www.tpwd.state.tx.us/publications/pwdpubs/media/pwd_bk_w700_0083.pdf

Stoll, R. J., Jr. and R.W. Donohoe. 1973. White-tailed deer harvest management in Ohio. Ohio Department of Natural Resources, Division of Wildlife, In Service Document 73.

Strole, T.A. and R.C. Anderson. 1992. White-tailed deer browsing: species preferences and implications for central Illinois forests. Natural Areas Journal 12:139-144.

Zagata, M.D. and A.O. Haugen. 1974. Influence of light and weather on observability of Iowa deer. Journal of Wildlife Management 38:220-228.

9.0 Supplemental Documents

9.1 Supplemental Document 1: Options available for white-tailed deer monitoring

To: Heartland Network Inventory and Monitoring Program
From: Paul M. Lukacs
Re: Options available for white-tailed deer monitoring
Date: May 2, 2005

Several options exist for ways to monitoring white-tailed deer abundance on National Park Service land within the Heartland Network. I will outline the pros and cons of four potential options for monitoring deer. I have listed the options we discussed during our April 26-28 meeting below.

1. Discontinue deer abundance monitoring and reallocate money elsewhere.
2. Use remote cameras as a means of collecting point transect distance sampling data.
3. Use mark-resight methods to estimate abundance.
4. Continue with the current road-based distance sampling surveys with minor modifications.

The first option is to discontinue the white-tailed deer surveys and use the money spent on these surveys elsewhere. The rationale for this option is based on the value of an estimate of deer abundance for the management of NPS lands given the small size of the properties in consideration. If we assume that the exact number of deer on a property is known at a point in time, how would we use that information for the management of deer? The management questions at hand include 1) how frequently do deer move off the park and onto neighboring private property and 2) is the deer population over-abundant and causing impacts on rare plants from feeding or trampling? Even if we knew the abundance of deer on a park exactly, that does not tell us how often deer are moving off the park nor what the deer do while they are off of the NPS property. It would require a telemetry study to obtain the information needed to answer that management question. On the same note, if we knew exactly how many deer were on a park; that would not provide information about how they are impacting rare plants. A study directly examining deer-plant interactions would be needed to answer that question. Therefore, it seems that monitoring deer abundance is not going to address the management issues at hand. This does not suggest that all studies of deer are not useful; I am merely suggesting that deer abundance is not the parameter that will help answer these questions. Based on this reasoning, I recommend discontinuing the deer abundance monitoring.

The second option is to use remote digital cameras to obtain distance sampling data. For this option, digital cameras would be set out at random locations throughout a park. A timer would be set to take a picture at set intervals throughout dawn and dusk. Flagging would mark distance bands out from each camera. The pictures would be reviewed and deer detected and there distances would be recorded. The data would be analyzed in a distance sampling framework to estimate deer density and abundance. This is a statistically valid method for obtaining a park-wide estimate of abundance. Potential problems with this method are 1) the initial cost of purchasing cameras which may be high; 2) image resolution may not be high enough to effectively detect deer; and 3) it is not known what the encounter rate will be at each camera. Approximately 60-80 detections of deer would be needed to obtain a reliable estimate of detection probability. An additional advantage of using remote cameras is the cameras could be used for more than just the deer surveys, thus defraying the initial investment.

The third option uses mark-resight techniques to estimate abundance of deer on each NPS property. This option requires that some deer be marked at each park. Deer would be captured by drop net and uniquely marked with a tag that could be read with binoculars or spotting scope. Marked deer are released. Surveys are conducted and the numbers of marked and unmarked deer are recorded along with the identification of marks if possible. The bulk of the surveys would be done from the tour road and a lesser effort would be done by walking through the unroaded portions of the park.

The amount of effort required and expected precision of the abundance estimate varies by the proportion of the deer population marked and the number of resighting surveys conducted. I will develop some estimates of effort and precision based on past deer surveys. At WICR, the estimated deer abundance is 312 individuals (SE=142). I will base the exploration of effort on the estimate of 312 deer. During a single night of the deer surveys approximately 100 deer or 30 percent of the population are seen each night. Therefore, I will define a resighting occasion as equal to the effort put into 3 trips around the tour road. I estimated the expected standard error from resighting effort ranging from 3-9 nights and number of marks in the population ranging from 30-90, representing marking between 10 and 30% of the population. The results of the exploration are given in Table 1.

Table 1. Expected standard errors for estimated abundance from a mark-resight survey at WICR.

Number	Resighting Occasions			
marked	3	5	7	9
30	52	38	32	28
60	32	25	20	18
90	24	18	15	14

As expected, standard error decreases with increasing effort. Standard error decreases more rapidly as the number of individuals marked increases, but the cost of marking individuals is likely to be greater than the cost of adding more resighting occasions. It should be noted that a standard error of 52 with an estimate of abundance of 312 yields a coefficient of variation of 17%. This is likely to be sufficiently precise to obtain a good estimate of trend in abundance after several years of data have been collected.

Several potential problems exist for mark-resight surveys. First, if movement rates of deer are relatively high, it is possible that many of the marked deer could leave the park and be unavailable for sampling. If this is the case, some deer would need to be fit with radio-collars to estimate the rate at which deer are moving. Second, marking deer is invasive. It is possible for deer to be injured or killed during tagging. Moreover, tags will be visible to park visitors and employees. Finally, marking deer is an expensive endeavor. Thus, while mark-resight methods can produce good estimates of abundance, it is not without its limitations.

It has been suggested to maintain the road-based distance sampling surveys during the resighting occasions. I do not recommend this for reasons beyond the inadequacy of road-based distance sampling. When searching for deer for a mark-resight survey, you want to maximize the number of deer detected regardless of their location. When surveying with distance sampling you want to be absolutely sure to see all deer along the transect prior to any movement. Thus, observers may be more likely to spend additional time search for deer away from the especially as they try to read tag numbers and therefore miss deer along the road or not see them until after they moved. Combining the mark-resight and distance sampling surveys would likely detract from both methods.

The fourth option is to continue the current road-based distance sampling with slight modifications to improve detection prior to movement. This method has only one advantage, namely it is cheap. There are numerous problems with road-based distance sampling. First, using roads as the sampling frame limits inference to the roads, so any inference to the entire park is by strong assumption only. Second, roads follow patterns in the geography of the park. This induces a correlation between the distribution of the transect and the distribution of the deer. This can cause the detection function to be invalid. When transects are not randomly placed, one must assume the deer are uniformly distributed with respect to the transect. We know this assumption will be false. Third, deer are rarely exactly on the road, therefore too few detections occur at zero distance. This makes fitting a detection function particularly difficult. We saw these problems expressed in the overview of the HTLN deer data at WICR and PERI. For these reasons, I simply cannot recommend continuing road-based distance sampling. While the road-based distance sampling is cheap, it is not useful.

9.2 Supplemental Document 2: Notes from the white-tailed deer breakout session, 3 August 2005, Hopewell Culture HNP

Notes from white-tailed deer breakout session
3 August 2005
Hopewell Culture NHP

Attendees: David Peitz (WICR), Gary Sullivan (WICR), Kevin Eads (PERI), Lisa Petit (CUVA), Kevin Skerl (CUVA), Jesse Bolli (HOME), Tim Breen (OZAR), Lloyd Morrison (WICR).

At HTLN parks where white-tailed deer have been designated as vital signs, the following issues associated with white-tailed deer were identified as important to park managers:

(1) General herd health and appearance.
(2) Collisions with vehicles on roads within and adjacent to park boundaries.
(3) Impacts on neighboring private lands (e.g., browsing in gardens, etc.), particularly as development increases in areas near parks.
(4) Impacts on park resources.

Discussion of these issues yielded the following insights:

(1) Lisa Petit, who is actively involved with deer management attempts at CUVA, stated that maintenance of herd health is not a sufficient reason for lethal removal of deer. Exceptions would be if deer exhibit signs of chronic wasting disease, high tick loads that could represent an increased threat of tick-borne diseases to humans, etc.
(2) Similarly, activities of deer on adjacent lands outside the parks are not sufficient reasons for managing deer populations within the parks.
(3) In general, there was low interest in obtaining data on movement of deer across park boundaries, or studying effects of deer outside the parks. Some limited radio-collar data has indicated that the majority of deer observed did not leave the park.
(4) No park manager was concerned about the current impact of deer on specific park resources.
(5) All park managers, however, were concerned that deer may have substantial impacts on park resources in the future, especially if they become more abundant, and that data on population trends over time would be very useful. Lisa Petit and Kevin Skerl suggested that the deer abundance issue at western parks in the network is analogous to the situation at CUVA (where deer are now a major problem) 25 years ago.

The possibility of dropping deer as a vital sign was raised, but there was little support for this. Most were of the opinion that vital signs should not be changed at this point.

There was a discussion of the different methods of estimating deer abundance, the problems associated with the distance method, and what methods other state and federal agencies were using. It was explained that a variety of methods may be used to estimate deer abundance, and some are more accurate than others; the more accurate methods require greater expenditures of time and effort. There was a discussion of what sort of burden of proof would be required in different types of circumstances, and an explanation of how the I&M program was attempting to "raise the bar" on the caliber of scientific work done in the parks. Lisa Petit and Kevin Skerl noted that if data are ever to be presented in a court of law, these data should be derived from widely used and accepted methods. It was pointed out that some methodologies currently in use are much more accurate than others.

The issue of how much our network could afford to invest in deer monitoring was raised, but no one present could definitively answer this question. The consensus of the managers was basically that *we should give them the best data we could with the resources available.*

There was a discussion of how to monitor impacts, and it was decided that conducting exclosure experiments was the best way to do this, although no one desired such information immediately. It was disclosed that ARPO and PERI have existing deer exclosures, and such exclosures also exist at the Springfield Nature Center, near WICR. It was pointed out that our network may not be able to increase the time and money spent on deer monitoring to conduct such experiments in the future. The managers seemed to think they could obtain resources from other sources or attract outside cooperators to conduct enclosure experiments, if necessary, although they deemed it very important to have background data on deer abundance trends to document any increases in the deer population.

The most important conclusions from this session were:

(1) Park managers are not so much concerned with absolute deer abundance in the parks as they are with changes in the relative abundance over time.
(2) Park managers, although concerned with the impacts of deer outside the park, felt such impacts were not the park's problem nor were such impacts sufficient for management of deer populations by lethal removal within the park.
(3) Park managers are more concerned about future potential impacts of white-tailed deer on park resources then any current impacts.

The following recommendations follow from this discussion:

(1) Continue monitoring white-tailed deer with similar methods as were employed last winter/spring (i.e., visual spotlighting surveys from the road at night). Do not use the distance method to estimate abundance or density. Rather, use simple counts of deer seen from the road as an *index* of deer abundance.

The perpendicular distance to individuals or herds can be recorded with GPS in order to map the location of deer. The map data will also be useful for defining the observable area. Further definition of the observable area can be accomplished with GIS using aerial photography, digital elevation maps, etc. By quantifying the area over which deer may generally be seen from the road, this will provide an *index* of density.

These measures would not be thought of as estimates of the actual deer abundance or density *per se* (as would be the case if one were using the distance method), but simple indices of these variables. These indices, however, would vary in direct proportion to the variables of interest, and would indicate whether deer populations were changing, and the general magnitude of the change. This would represent the minimum information deemed necessary by park managers for which deer were designated as vital signs.

(2) Infrequently (every 3-5 years, depending upon budget or other considerations), mark-recapture or other methods could be employed to obtain more accurate estimates of deer abundance or density. This *double sampling* approach would allow us to determine correlations between the annual index of deer populations with the more accurate abundance data determined from other methods. Ultimately, it should be possible to estimate deer abundances with relatively good accuracy in years when only index data from visual surveys are available.

9.3 Supplemental Document 3: Recommendations for conducting white-tailed deer surveys

Recommendations for conducting white-tailed deer surveys

by Dr. Lloyd Morrison, HTLN Quantitative Ecologist

The suggested approach to white-tailed deer monitoring, resulting from a discussion with resource managers of the appropriate parks at the 2005 annual meeting, was to count deer visible from park roads in drive-through surveys.[1] This will yield an *index* of the *relative abundance* of deer, which should be correlated to some unknown degree with the absolute abundance, but will allow detection of general increases or decreases in the actual population over time. Because the number of deer observed in such surveys is strongly dependent upon their *activity*, and deer activity is influenced by many factors, it is critical to conduct the surveys in such a way as to minimize as much of this *variability* as possible. The greater the variability inherent in the data set, the less likely we will be to detect any real trends in population density, particularly using this index of relative abundance.

In pilot work at WICR, three surveys were conducted back-to-back in a ~3 hour period (~1 hr per survey), and this was repeated on three consecutive days (or nights), for a total of 9 surveys. (Surveys could be conducted during the day or at night; it doesn't matter which, but whatever is decided should be used for all parks, and throughout the monitoring program.) The problem with conducting multiple, back-to-back surveys within several hours of each other is that one is likely to see the same deer, in the same place, doing the same thing in two or more surveys. Thus, back-to-back surveys do not represent true replicates, but rather *pseudoreplicates*, because they are not independent.

Thus, in the example of three back-to-back surveys per day, on three different days, only three of the nine surveys would be independent (one from each day). For any data analyses requiring independent observations, the sample size would have to be 3 rather than 9. It would be problematic to use all 9 surveys even for descriptive statistics such as calculating mean and variance. The variance would likely be underestimated if all 9 were used, because the counts taken on the same day are likely to be more similar than counts taken on different days.

My recommendation is to conduct only one survey in a 24-hour period. One could then make the reasonable assumption that the counts are independent. The total number of replicate counts that should be done for each park in each year will depend upon funding and logistics. Three counts should be regarded as minimum, but the more counts that are made, the greater the reduction in sample variance, and the more powerful our surveys will be to detect any trends.

To minimize variability due to deer *activity* or *behavior* in relation to environmental variables, surveys should always be done during the same time of day (or night). An acceptable range of *climatic* conditions should be defined, and surveys should not be conducted outside these conditions. For example, a range of acceptable temperatures should be decided upon, and surveys should not be conducted in unusually warm or cold weather. Likewise, surveys should not be conducted during 'inclement' weather, such as rain, snow, high winds, etc. If surveys are to be conducted at night, they should be standardized by the phase of the moon (e.g., always conducted during the full moon). If surveys are to be conducted during moonlit nights, cloud

---

[1] *Notes from white-tailed deer breakout session*, 3 August 2005, Hopewell Culture NHP

cover would also have to be taken into effect. When any environmental variables exceed the acceptable ranges or thresholds previously decided upon, the survey for that particular day (or night) should be aborted, and rescheduled for the following day (or night).

To minimize *inter-observer bias*, the same observers should be used for the surveys on each occasion, in each park, in each year, and in succeeding years to the extent possible, given the unavoidable turnover in NPS personnel over time. If distances from the road to the deer are to be determined with rangefinders for the purpose of constructing maps, observers should be properly trained in the use of the rangefinders prior to conducting the actual surveys. This could be done by setting up targets at known distances and training observers until their accuracy is within a reasonable, predetermined interval.

9.4 Supplemental Document 4: 2005 White-tailed deer counts by time after official sunset

2005 White-tailed deer counts by time after official sunset.

Park	1-hr	2-hr	3-hr
Arkansas Post National Memorial			
Day 1	22	19	31
Day 2	28	25	30
Day 3	24	26	28
Pea Ridge National Military Park			
Day 1	35	22	21
Day 2	46	41	29
Day 3	64	50	52
Wilson's Creek National Battlefield			
Day 1	55	33	32
Day 2	32	34	N/A
Day 3	43	24	15

10.0 Standard Operating Procedures

White-tailed Deer Monitoring Protocol for the Heartland Network Inventory and Monitoring Program

10.1 Standard Operating Procedure 1: Before the Field Season

Version 1.00 (August 2007)

Revision History Log:

Prev. Version #	Revision Date	Author	Changes Made	Reason for Change	New Version #

This Standard Operating Procedure (SOP) gives step-by-step instructions on how to prepare for white-tailed deer monitoring on National Park Service lands within the Heartland Network Inventory and Monitoring Program. Prior to each field season, usually beginning in November or December of the preceding year, all field crew personnel should review this entire protocol, including SOPs.

I. General Preparation and Review

Procedures:

1. Refreshing deer identification skills is particularly important, as is reviewing all standard surveying procedures. Deer identification skills are best honed at night with the aid of a spotlight. Locating an object such as a deer eye at night with a spotlight can be difficult, with proficiency gained through practice and experience. State game and fish laws, however, prohibit spotlighting deer without approval from law enforcement officials with jurisdiction over the area. Get approval from law enforcement before practicing any spotlighting of deer.

2. The use of a rangefinder to measure distances to deer can be particularly difficult at night and should be practiced before the start of the field season. Observer skills with the rangefinder should be checked periodically during surveys with reflectors set at predetermined distances from the survey vehicle.

3. Observers should also practice estimating distances to objects, especially those less than 20 m, a distance too close for most rangefinders to take a reading.

4. Maps of the survey routes in each park should be printed and each crew member should become familiar with the routes and habitat types to be encountered prior to entering the field.

5. A field notebook for the survey year should be prepared with pages for entry of sampling schedules, observer names, field hours, and unique happenings that may influence how data is reported. Information included in trip reports is based on what is recorded in field notebooks, so it is imperative that they are clearly organized for ease of field note entry.

II. Scheduling Field Work

Procedures:

1. White-tailed deer surveys should begin no sooner than the first week of January and extend no later than the second full week of March, unless inclement weather delays surveys and field conditions allow for a later sampling date. Inclement weather and personnel workloads will preclude the scheduling of sampling events to specific annual dates. Sampling dates should be scheduled and logistics arranged prior to the start of the field season.
2. Surveys should be scheduled for nights with wind speeds less than 30 km/hr (18.6 m/hr), rain less than heavy (visibility and hearing impaired), snow fall less than moderate (visibility impaired), and visibility greater than 3.2 km (two miles) (Bates 2004). Visibility can be obtained at: http://www.wunderground.com/.
3. Monitoring efforts at Arkansas Post National Monument, Arkansas (ARPO), Pea Ridge National Military Park, Arkansas (PERI) and Wilson's Creek National Battlefield, Missouri (WICR) require at minimum three field days at each to complete. However, six field days at each park should be scheduled. One field day at each park should be scheduled each week during the sampling window, January – March.
4. Three deer surveys, the first starting one hour after official sunset and the remaining two each consecutive hour thereafter, should be scheduled each night.
5. Visibility estimates should be taken on the first survey day as soon as the last deer survey has been completed.

III. Organizing Supplies and Equipment

Procedures:

1. An equipment list should be compiled and equipment organized and made ready several weeks in advance of the field season. This allows time to make needed repairs and order equipment. The following is a list of field equipment needed for one survey crew.

Table 1.01. Field equipment list for conducting white-tailed deer surveys on National Park Service lands within the Heartland Network Inventory and Monitoring Program.

Number Required	Description
4	1,000,000 candlelight spotlight (two are held in reserve as spares)
1	Clipboard
2	Yardage Pro 1000 Rangefinder
3	Pencil
1	Jeep
1	Kestrel 4000 pocket weather tracker
2	Land measure compass mounted on poster board
1	Global Positioning System with data entry forms loaded into the data dictionary
1	Pin flag for determining wind direction
1	Spotlight splitter cable
1	Compass
6	Illuminated reflectors on 36 in. rods
1	First Aid Kit

2. Copies of field data sheets should be made prior to entering the field. Approximately 25 % of all field data forms should be made on write-in-the-rain paper. See Appendix A for data entry forms.

IV. References

Bates, S. 2004. White-tailed deer density monitoring protocol version 1.0: distance and pellet group surveys. National Capital Region Network Inventory and Monitoring Program, Washington, D.C., USA.

White-tailed Deer Monitoring Protocol for the Heartland Network Inventory and Monitoring Program

10.2 Standard Operating Procedure 2: Training Observers

Version 1.00 (August 2007)

Revision History Log:

Prev. Version #	Revision Date	Author	Changes Made	Reason for Change	New Version #

This Standard Operating Procedure (SOP) gives step-by-step instructions on how to train observers for white-tailed deer monitoring on National Park Service lands within the Heartland Network Inventory and Monitoring Program. All observers must learn to (1) identify deer in the field at night; (2) estimate or measure (using a rangefinder) distances to deer at night; and (3) estimate visibility during surveys. Special skills required to operate and record data using a Global Positioning System (GPS) are covered in SOP #3 "Using the Global Positioning System", SOP #5 "Conducting the Spotlight Survey" and SOP #6 "Establishing Visibility during Surveys" and should be practiced before entering the field.

I. Conducting the Spotlight Survey

The most essential component for the collection of credible, high-quality deer data is well-trained and experienced observers. This cannot be overemphasized. Proficient observers will identify and count all but the most difficult to see deer within a survey area.

Procedures:

1. Beginning several months prior to the field season, practice deer identification skills, especially at night using a 1,000,000 candle power spotlight.
2. In the absence of actual deer, blue-green reflectors placed in various habitat types can be used to hone identification skills. Observers should be able to locate and ID more than 90% of deer or reflectors spotted by the observer group as a whole. All but the most difficult to observe deer or reflectors should be spotted.
3. Working as a group of two or more observers, determine the number of deer in a defined area of observation and the number of deer each observer saw. All observers should practice together until all observers report seeing more than 90 % of the group's total deer count.
4. A working knowledge of the reflective characteristics of all animal eyes likely to be encountered during a survey should be gained prior to the start of surveys to avoid misidentifying other animals as deer.

5. Regardless of skill level, observers should spend time in the field identifying deer at night prior to starting a survey. Deer identification skills should be practiced during different light conditions (i.e., full moon, new moon, cloud cover, etc.) and weather if possible.

II. Measuring Distance with a Rangefinder

A necessary element for accurately mapping the location of deer is skill in measuring the distance from the survey vehicle to each deer or deer group. The distance and angle from the observation point recorded in the GPS (i.e., the vehicle) to the deer is used to map deer locations.

Procedures:

1. Beginning several months prior to the field-season, practice measuring distances to various objects with a rangefinder, especially at night with illumination from a 1,000,000 candle power spotlight. Proper positioning of the spotlight when obtaining measures with a rangefinder is critical.
2. Reflectors placed at known distances in various habitats to be encountered during surveys aids in training observers to distinguish if they have gotten an accurate measurement or not. Erroneous measures can occur at night if the laser from the rangefinder hits an unnoticed object between the observer and a deer or deer group. Therefore a general ability to estimate distances serves as a check for actual measured distances.
3. Maps of the parks to be surveyed need to be reviewed for observers to familiarize themselves with each park and give them a general idea of distances to land features found along the survey route.

III. Establishing Visibility during Surveys

Determining the area surveyed for white-tailed deer is critical for obtaining an accurate estimate of deer density in the survey area. Therefore, each observer spotlighting deer must be equally skilled in determining the distance at which they can no longer effectively spot a deer.

Procedures:

1. While practicing both spotlighting and distance measuring skills, each observer should also spend time taking distance measures out to a point were visibility with a spotlight has diminished to a level were deer can no longer be effectively spotted. This distance varies with habitat type. Visibility distances are generally much closer in wooded areas than open fields.
2. The maximum distance measured in open areas should be no greater than 250 m. Therefore, observers should practice taking measurements at distances less than 250 m.

White-tailed Deer Monitoring Protocol for the Heartland Network Inventory and Monitoring Program

10.3 Standard Operating Procedure 3: Using the Global Positioning System

Please see: http://www1.nature.nps.gov/im/units/htln/datamanagement.cfm.

White-tailed Deer Monitoring Protocol for the Heartland Network Inventory and Monitoring Program

10.4 Standard Operating Procedure 4: Establishing Survey Routes

Version 1.00 (August 2007)

Revision History Log:

Prev. Version #	Revision Date	Author	Changes Made	Reason for Change	New Version #

This Standard Operating Procedure (SOP) gives step-by-step instructions on how to establish survey routes for white-tailed deer monitoring on National Park Service lands within the Heartland Network Inventory and Monitoring Program. Survey routes have already been established at Wilson's Creek National Battlefield, Missouri, Pea Ridge National Military Park, Arkansas, and Arkansas Post National Memorial, Arkansas (see section 2.2, spatial design), and will not change over time. Thus this SOP is primarily relevant to other parks at which deer monitoring may be initiated.

I. Selecting Survey Routes

It is desirable for survey routes to pass through as many habitat types within a park as exist to obtain a relatively accurate estimate of deer numbers in the park. If possible, the amount of each habitat surveyed should be in proportion to their presence within a park. It is also important to select survey routes from existing all-weather roads for safety reasons and so that inclement weather will not prevent sampling for extended periods of time. It will be the program leader's responsibility to select and plan survey routes.

Procedure:

1. Using the latest imagery of a park, select all hard service roads for consideration as potential survey routes.
2. If possible, select survey routes that traverse a park in one continuous survey. Try to minimize the need to backtrack over areas already surveyed. While segmented survey routes will work, they are not as efficient as continuous survey routes for sampling deer and extra care needs to be taken during surveys to ensure an accurate measure of the survey route length is obtained.
3. Because of the small size of most parks to be monitored, every all-weather road should be included in the survey as long as no area is sampled multiple times during the same survey. The area covered from the survey route should represent at least 10

% of the total area of a park if possible. In many cases more than 10 % of a park is covered. (In a park such as Pea Ridge National Military Park, however, this is not the case; approximately 6.5 % of the main unit of the park is covered annually.)

4. Select survey routes that can be closed to the public during spotlight surveys. Usually this will not be an issue as park operational hours keep visitors out of the park during the nighttime survey period.

5. Once survey routes have been determined, maps need to be made and taken to the field to guide crews surveying deer. Survey routes should be overlaid on the most current imagery of a park to aid surveyors in familiarizing themselves with a park and in identifying areas more likely to hold deer.

White-tailed Deer Monitoring Protocol for the Heartland Network Inventory and Monitoring Program

10.5 Standard Operating Procedure 5: Conducting the Spotlight Survey

Version 1.00 (August 2007)

Revision History Log:

Prev. Version #	Revision Date	Author	Changes Made	Reason for Change	New Version #

This Standard Operating Procedure (SOP) gives step-by-step instructions on how to conduct white-tailed deer surveys on National Park Service lands within the Heartland Network Inventory and Monitoring Program (HTLN). The procedures for: 1) collecting data, 2) logging data on a Global Positioning System unit, and 3) filling out paper data forms are covered in this SOP.

I. Conducting the Spotlight Survey

Spotlight deer counts are used to establish an index of white-tailed deer population density for the area surveyed on each HTLN park unit. From pilot data, it was observed that the highest number of deer counted each night at Wilson's Creek National Battlefield and Pea Ridge National Military Park generally occurred in the first hour following official sunset (See Supplemental Document #4). At Arkansas Post National Memorial, however, the maximum number of deer counted occurred in the third replicate. Therefore, three surveys commencing one hour after official sunset will be used to count deer numbers each night. Jester and Dillard (2001) and Shult and Armstrong (1983) recommend starting surveys one hour after official sunset to maximize deer observed. One deer survey should be conducted each week for six consecutive weeks on each HTLN park unit if possible. A four person crew is needed to survey deer: a driver, a person to record and log data, and two people to spot deer and measure angles and distances.

Procedures:

1. Prior to the start of a survey, determine the route to be surveyed and start time (see SOP #4 "Establishing Survey Routes" for details on establishing a survey route). Surveys should start one hour after official sunset.

2. Surveys are conducted from a survey vehicle moving no more then 16 km/hr (10 m/hr) using two 1,000,000 candlepower spotlights. One observer with a spotlight needs to be positioned on each side of the survey vehicle and count deer on their respective side of the vehicle. Stop the survey vehicle as soon as a deer or deer group is spotted. The vehicle should remain stopped until all data is logged and a count of the number of deer at that location is made. Deer are counted with the vehicle stopped so that deer in close proximity to the group being counted are not included in that group but in their own group count. Use visual cues such as deer repeatedly looking at each other or by nearest neighbor criterion to partition deer into their respective groups. If a deer is less than half the distance from the closest deer or deer group than it is from the next closest deer or deer group, then it should be grouped with the first deer or deer group.
3. All deer seen along the survey route are counted and their location recorded using GPS technologies. Distances from the stopped survey vehicle to all deer or deer groups are determined with a rangefinder or, for deer < 20 m from the vehicle, by visual estimates. Deer are usually observed in groups, in which case distance is taken or estimated to the center-most deer in the group.
4. In order to map locations of deer, the direction (i.e., left front, left back, right front, right back) and angle (measured with a land measure compass) of all deer or deer groups from the survey vehicle are recorded.
5. Navigate the survey route slowly trying to maintain a constant speed during the survey. Adjust speed of the survey vehicle only slightly as the terrain dictates. Slow down if observers are unable to effectively sample their assigned survey area.
6. If during a count, high wind or heavy rains occur, cease the count and wait until the weather improves or else cancel sampling for that day and try again on a later date. These conditions inhibit deer activity and impair one's ability to detect deer. Counts should not be conducted if sustained wind speeds increase to greater than 30 km/hr (18.6 m/hr), if it is raining hard (visibility and hearing is impaired) or snowing.

II. Entering data on a Global Positioning System (GPS) unit

Procedures:

1. Prior to the first day in the field, load the DeerSurveyVer3.ddf data dictionary onto the GPS unit. Steps on how to download data onto the GPS unit can be found in SOP #3 "Using the Global Positioning System".
2. One half hour before the count begins, install the GPS unit inside the jeep. Do this by first assembling the magnetic mount, poles, and Hurricane antenna together and then place it in the center of the jeep. Next attach the cable that runs from the Hurricane antenna to the GPS unit (Trimble GeoXT). Make sure the GPS unit is on before plugging the cable in.

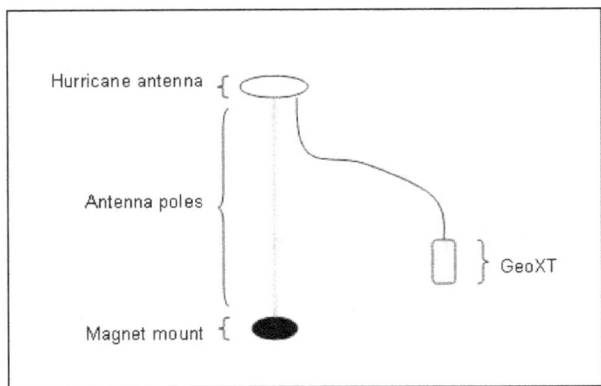

Figure 5.01. Diagram of antenna assembly.

3. On the GPS unit open the program TerraSync. Check the GPS unit settings, such as coordinate system, antenna options, and Max. PDOP which should be set to 6 (see SOP #3 pages 20 – 25 on how to do this).

4. Once TerraSync is setup, create a new file by opening the data window and selecting new. In the field choices select the following:

File Type: Rover
Location: Default
Dictionary Name: DeerSurveyVer3
File Name: The file name must match the file name recorded on the paper data form and include the Park Code (4 digits), year (4 digits), "deer" to identify the project and the survey number (#) 1, 2 or 3 (ex. wicr2007deer1).

After the fields are filled out click Create.

5. A new window is now open. Click on the Options drop down menu and select Log Later. Now highlight the Deer Location choice and click Create. This opens the DeerSurveyVer3 data dictionary. Notice that the pause icon is flashing at the top of the screen; this means it is not collecting feature positions. When it is time to collect a deer location click the Log button. Notice that the pause icon turns into a pencil with a number to the right of it. The number indicates the amount of feature positions being collected for each deer location. Fifty (50) feature positions should be captured for each deer location. The data dictionary fields get filled out with the same attributes as the field sheet. The fields in the data dictionary are either pull down menus (▼) or numeric fields. When you click in a menu field a list will open. Choose the correct term from this list. To populate the numeric fields click the keyboard icon at the bottom of the screen, this will open a numeric keyboard. After all fields are filled out and at least 50 feature positions collected click OK. Repeat procedure 5 until all deer observations for the count are completed.

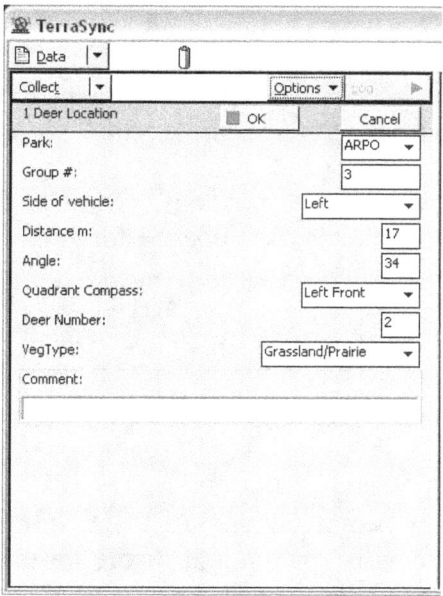

Figure 5.02. Screen capture of the deer survey data dictionary.

6. After the survey is complete click Close and then Yes to the question: Close this file. Are you sure? If no more surveys are to be done in the same evening close TerraSync and turn off the GPS unit.
7. Once all counts are completed for a park see SOP #3 for transferring, correcting and exporting data, SOP #7 "Geospatial Data Management", and SOP #8 "Data Management" on managing the data.

III. Filling out the Paper Data Form

When observers are conducting a deer survey they should fill out a copy of the field data form "Spotlight Survey Form" (an example is located at the end of this SOP) as a check for data logged on the GPS unit. The paper data form also serves as the only record for general survey information (recorded at the top of the data form), as this is not logged with the GPS unit. The paper form is filled out simultaneously with the logging of deer location data, so additional field time is not required to accomplish this task.

Procedures:

1. Fill out the general information prior to starting the survey.
2. While recording the start time, record the starting weather conditions, cloud cover, and moon illumination.
3. Once a survey has begun, record all deer seen and the angle and distance to each individual deer or deer group.
4. At the end of each survey record the ending time, weather conditions, and cloud cover.
5. The following is a complete list with descriptors for each variable that needs to be filled out:

GPS File Name (aaaaYYYYdeer#): Write in the Park Code (4 digits), year (4 digits), "deer" to identify the project, and Count # (1, 2 or 3). The GPS File Name recorded on a data sheet must correspond to its associated file name on the GPS unit.

Date (mm/dd/yyyy): Write in the month (2 digits), day (2 digits), and year (4 digits) in the format shown for the day a count is being conducted. Include the forward slash. Example 07/19/2003

Park: Write the appropriate Park Code (ARPO, PERI or WICR).

Route: Write a short descriptor identifying the survey route for which a count is being taken within a park (i.e., Tour Road).

Observer Initials: Fill in the three initials of each person conducting the count using capital letters. If someone does not have a middle name, put an underscore for their middle initial. Examples would be DGP for David G. Peitz or JTC for J. Tyler Cribbs. In the database, these initials will correspond to the full name and contact information for that person (the 3-character initials in the database must be unique, and if two people have the same initials, one should be given an honorary middle name).

Starting time (hhmm): Write in the time to the nearest minute when the deer count begins, using the hour and minute format shown. Use military time (add 12 to the hour beginning with 1 pm through 11 pm). Fill in all four digits. Examples are 1630 (4:30 pm) and 1900 (7:00 pm).

End time (hhmm): Write in the time to the nearest minute when the deer count ends, using the hour and minute format shown. Use military time.

Beginning and Ending:
> **Temperature (°C):** Record the ambient temperature during the start and end of a count in degrees Celsius, to one decimal place or rounded off to the nearest degree. Use a Kestrel 4000 pocket weather tracker to record ambient temperatures.
>
> **Humidity (%):** Record the percent (%) relative humidity during the start and end of a count using a Kestrel 4000 pocket weather tracker.
>
> **Wind Speed (m/s):** Record the wind speed in meters/second during the start and end of a count using a Kestrel 4000 pocket weather tracker.
>
> **Wind Direction (°):** Using a pin flag and compass, determine the direction in degrees (0-359°) the wind is moving, and record this direction. The direction the wind is moving is recorded at the start and end of each count.

Precipitation: Record the Rain Code (0 - 5) from the following Table 5.01 as it applies to precipitation observed during the start and end of a count.

Table 5.01. Codes used to record precipitation type during deer surveys.

Rain Code	Explanation
0	no rain
1	mist or light fog
2	light drizzle
3	light rain
4	heavy rain; difficult to hear, visibility impaired (discontinue survey)
5	snow or heavy fog (discontinue survey)

Moon Illumination: Determine percent moon illumination at the time a survey will begin. Percent moon illumination can be found at: http://imagiware.com/astro/moon.cgi.

Starting and Ending Cloud Cover (0 - 7): Estimate the percent cover of clouds during the start and end of the deer survey. Cover is estimated within modified Daubenmire cover classes (Table 5.02). If there are patches of clouds in different areas of the sky, try to imagine gathering them together in one part of the sky and recording what cover class that would represent.

Table 5.02. Cloud cover estimates within modified Daubenmire cover classes.

Cover class	Explanation
0	None present
1	0 – 1 % cloud coverage
2	1 – 5 % cloud coverage
3	5 – 25 % cloud coverage
4	25 – 50 % cloud coverage
5	50 – 75 % cloud coverage
6	75 – 95 % cloud coverage
7	95 – 100 % cloud coverage

Group # Assigned: Record sequentially, a unique number identifying each deer or deer group observed during a count. Generally, numbering begins with one (1) and increases as needed for each deer or deer group observed.

Side of Vehicle: Using a side of vehicle code, record on which side of the road each deer or deer group is observed (i.e., "L" for left, "R" for right, "OR" for on road).

Distance (m): Using a rangefinder, measure and record the distance from the observer to the deer or deer group. If a group of deer are spotted, take one distance measure to the center-most individual in the group.

Angle (°): Using a land measure compass, record the angle of each deer or deer group from the survey vehicle. Angles are measured from 0 to 90° in each quadrant of the vehicle. Deer located on the transect line will have an angle of 0° and should be placed in the quadrant they moved from if known or can be reasonably assumed. Deer located at an angle of 90° from the survey vehicle should be placed in the quadrant they moved from if known or can be reasonably assumed.

Quadrant: Using quadrant codes, record the quadrant each deer or deer group is located in relation to the survey vehicle (i.e., "LF" for left front, "LB" for left back, "RF" for right front, "RB" for right back).

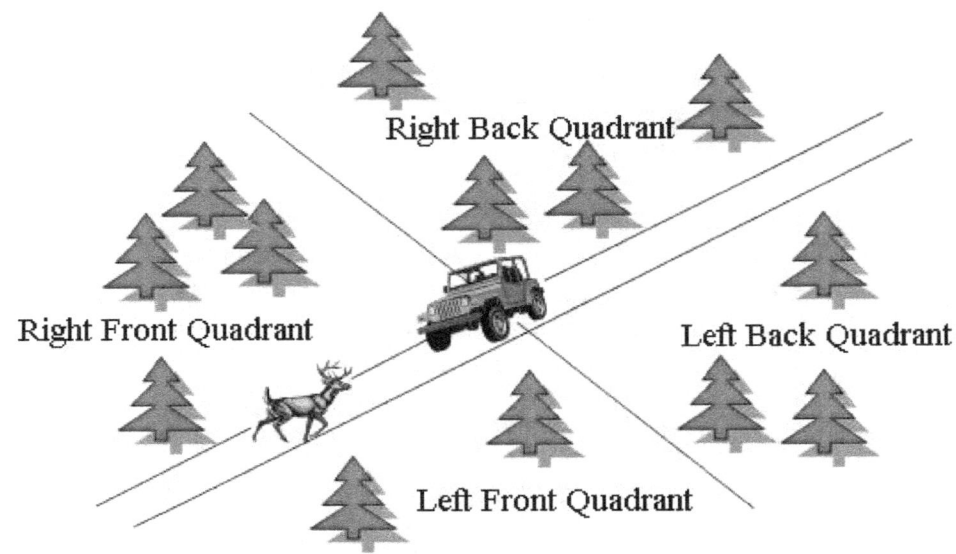

Figures 5.03. Deer shown would be recorded with an angle of 0° and a quadrant code of "RF" because it can be reasonably assumed that the deer is moving from the right front quadrant of the vehicle into the left front quadrant.

Number of Deer: Record the number of deer seen every time a deer (1 individual) or deer group (2 or more individuals) is observed.

Habitat Type: Using habitat type codes, record the habitat type in which each deer or deer group is observed. Table 5.03 list habitat type codes.

Table 5.03. Codes used to record habitat type during deer surveys.

Habitat Type Code	Explanation
SAV	Savanna
GRP	Grassland/Prairie
UPS	Upland scrub
UPF	Upland forest
RIG	Riparian grassland
RIS	Riparian scrub
RIF	Riparian forest
MOL	Mowed lawn
OTH	Other

IV. References

Jester S. and J. Dillard. 2001. Conducting white-tailed deer spotlight surveys in the cross-timbers and prairie region of north and central Texas. http://www.tpwd.state.tx.us/publications/pwdpubs/media/pwd_rp_w7000_1126.pdf.

Shult, M.J. and B. Armstrong. 1983. Deer census techniques. http://www.tpwd.state.tx.us/publications/pwdpubs/media/pwd_bk_w700_0083.pdf

Spotlight Survey Form

Field Data Form – White-tailed deer spotlight survey data form

Date: ___/___/___ Park: _____ Route: _____ Observers: _____ GPS File Name: _____

Start Time: _____ End Time: _____

Beginning: Temperature: _____ °C Humidity: _____ % Wind: _____ m/s Wind Direction: _____ ° Precipitation: 0 1 2 3 4 5

Ending: Temperature: _____ °C Humidity: _____ % Wind: _____ m/s Wind Direction: _____ ° Precipitation: 0 1 2 3 4 5

Starting Cloud Cover: 0 1 2 3 4 5 6 7 Ending Cloud Cover: 0 1 2 3 4 5 6 7 Moon Illumination: _____ %

Group # assigned	Side of vehicle	Distance (m)	Angle (°)	Quadrant	Number of deer	Habitat type	Comments

Spotlight Survey Form: Categories, Definitions and Descriptions.

Codes used to record precipitation and cloud cover, as well as side of vehicle, quadrant and habitat type a deer is observed in during white-tailed deer surveys.

Rain Code	Explanation	Cloud Cover Code	Explanation	Side of Vehicle Code	Explanation	Quadrant Code	Explanation	Habitat Type Code	Explanation
0	No rain	0	None present	L	Left side of vehicle	LF	Left Front	SAV	Savanna
1	Mist or light fog	1	Trace – 1 %	R	Right side of vehicle	LB	Left Back	GRP	Grassland/Prairie
2	Light drizzle	2	1 – 5 %	OR	On Road	RF	Right Front	UPS	Upland scrub
3	Light rain	3	5 – 25 %			RB	Right Back	UPF	Upland forest
4	Heavy rain; difficult to hear	4	25 – 50 %					RIG	Riparian grassland
5	Snow or heavy fog	5	50 – 75 %					RIS	Riparian scrub
		6	75 – 95 %					RIF	Riparian forest
		7	95 – 100 %					MOL	Mowed lawn
								OTH	Other

10.6 Standard Operating Procedure 6: Establishing Visibility during Surveys

Version 1.00 (August 2007)

Revision History Log:

Prev. Version #	Revision Date	Author	Changes Made	Reason for Change	New Version #

This Standard Operating Procedure (SOP) gives step-by-step instructions on how to establish visibility, i.e., the area in which a deer might be seen during surveys. The procedures for: 1) collecting data, 2) logging data on a Global Positioning System unit, and 3) filling out paper data forms are covered in this SOP.

I. Establishing Visibility during Surveys

Determining the area surveyed for white-tailed deer is critical for obtaining an accurate estimate of deer density in the survey area. The following procedures describe how to estimate the amount of area surveyed across habitats using visibility measures taken with a spotlight and rangefinder. Visibility measures are taken on the first survey night after the deer counts are completed by recording the perpendicular distances from the survey vehicle to a point beyond which deer would not be visible. A four person crew is needed to measure visibility: a driver, a person to record and log data, and two people to measure perpendicular distances. Observers measuring perpendicular distances must be the same two individuals who conducted the deer count that night.

Procedures:

1. As soon as deer counts are completed, starting at the beginning of the survey route, measure visibility on each side of the survey vehicle every 0.16 km (1/10th mile). In an attempt to get a more robust picture of how much area is being surveyed along the route, the location of the survey vehicle should be adjusted slightly if objects are encountered that block the true area observed during a survey. For example, if the view of an open field is blocked by a single cedar tree in the ditch next to the survey vehicle, move the vehicle forward or backward to see the field.

2. At each 0.16 km (1/10th mile) stopping point, use a rangefinder to measure the perpendicular distance at which an observer can no longer discern what they are seeing with a spotlight, especially if it is a deer. Estimate the distance if it is less than 20 m. In areas were visibility is good, such as an open field, record visibility measures out to 250 m but no further. Deer are rarely discernible at this distance even under ideal field conditions.
3. The location each perpendicular measure is taken is marked with a GPS unit.
4. Using GIS technologies, perpendicular distances are plotted on a map, a polygon is created, and the survey area determined. SOP #7 "Geospatial Data Management" details how to determine the size of a survey area.

II. Entering data on a Global Positioning System (GPS) unit

Procedures:

1. Prior to the first day in the field, load the DeerVisibility.ddf data dictionary onto the GPS unit. Steps on how to download data onto the GPS can be found in SOP #3 "Using the Global Positioning System".
2. Before the visibility estimate begins, install the GPS unit inside the jeep. Do this by first assembling the magnetic mount, poles, and Hurricane antenna together and then place them in the center of the jeep. Next attach the cable that runs from the Hurricane antenna to the GPS unit (Trimble GeoXT). Make sure the GPS unit is on before plugging the cable in.

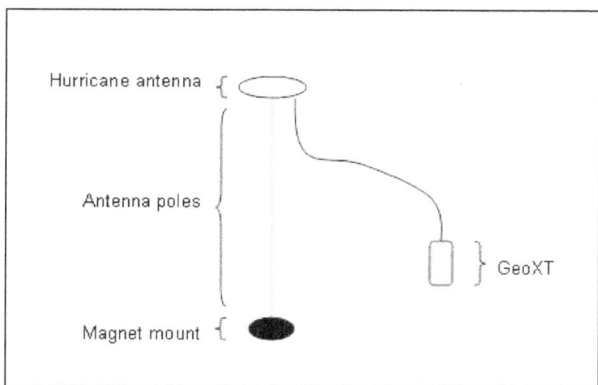

Figure 6.01. Diagram of antenna assembly.

3. On the GPS unit open the program TerraSync. Check the GPS unit settings, such as coordinate system, antenna options, and Max. PDOP which should be set to 6 (see SOP #3 pages 20 – 25 on how to do this).
4. Once TerraSync is setup, create a new file by opening the data window and selecting new. In the field choices select the following:

File Type: Rover
Location: Default
Dictionary Name: DeerVisibility

File Name: The file name must match the file name recorded on the paper data form and include the Park Code (4 digits), year (4 digits), "deer" to identify the project, the survey number (#) 1, 2 or 3 and "vis" to identify this file as containing visibility measures (ex. wicr2007deer1vis).

After the fields are filled out click Create.

5. A new window is now open. Click on the Options drop down menu and select Log Now. Now highlight the VisibilityDeer choice and click Create. This opens the DeerVisibility data dictionary. Notice that the pencil icon is flashing at the top of the screen; this means it is collecting feature positions. The number indicates the amount of feature positions being collected for each visibility location. Fifty (50) feature positions should be captured for each visibility location. The data dictionary fields get filled out with the same attributes as the field sheet. The "Mile tenth" field populates itself, increasing a tenth for each new visibility point collected. The Right Distance and Left Distance fields are numeric. To populate the numeric fields click the keyboard icon at the bottom of the screen this will open a numeric keyboard. Input the distance that the observers tell you. After all fields are filled out and at least 50 feature positions collected click OK. Repeat this step until all visibility observations are complete.

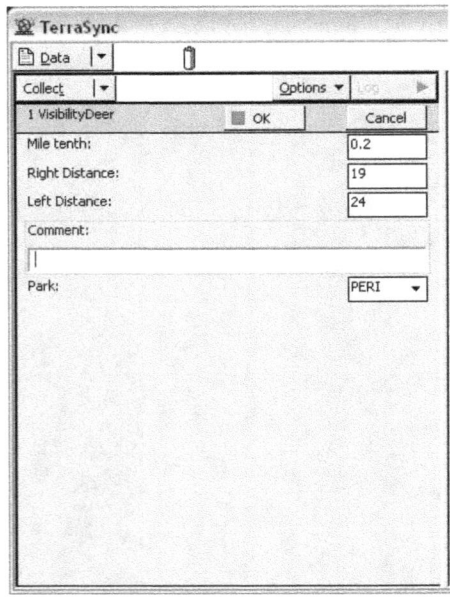

Figure 6.02. Screen capture of the deer visibility data dictionary.

6. After the visibility estimate is complete click Close and then Yes to the question: Close this file. Are you sure? If no more visibility estimates are to be done in the same evening close TerraSync and turn off the GPS unit. If another visibility estimate is to be done create a new file and repeat steps 4 – 6.

7. Once all visibility estimates are completed for a park see SOP #3 for transferring, correcting, and exporting data, and SOP #7 "Geospatial Data Management" on managing the data.

III. Filling out the Paper Data Form

Procedures:

1. When observers are determining visibility in the survey area, they should fill out a copy of the field data form "Visibility Estimates for Spotlight Survey" (an example is located at the end of this SOP) as a check for data logged on the GPS unit. The paper form also serves as the only record for general survey information (recorded at the top of the data form), as this information this is not logged with the GPS unit. The paper form is filled out simultaneously with the logging of GPS point data, so additional field time is not required to accomplish this task.
2. Fill out the general information prior to starting the survey.
3. Record the start time, starting odometer reading, date, observers, route and GPS file name.
4. Record the left and right perpendicular distances at each 0.16 km (1/10th mile) interval as they are being logged with the GPS unit.
5. At the end of each survey, record the ending time and ending odometer reading.
6. The following is a complete list with descriptors for each variable that needs to be filled out when observers are determining visibility along a survey route.

   Date (mm/dd/yyyy): Write in the month (2 digits), day (2 digits), and year (4 digits) in the format shown for the day a visibility survey is being conducted. Include forward slashes. Example 07/19/2003

   Park: Write the appropriate Park Code (ARPO, PERI, or WICR).

   Route: Write a short descriptor identifying the survey route visibility is being measured along within a park (i.e., Tour Road).

   Observers: Fill in the three initials of each crew member conducting the visibility measures using capital letters. Examples would be DGP for David G. Peitz or JTC for J. Tyler Cribbs. If someone does not have a middle name put an underscore for their middle initial. In the database, these initials will correspond to the full name and contact information for that person (the 3-character initials in the database must be unique, and if two people have the same initials, one should be given an honorary middle name).

   Beginning Odometer Reading (miles): Record the vehicle's odometer reading to the 1/10th mile (0.16 km) at the beginning of the visibility survey.

   Ending Odometer Reading (miles): Record the vehicle's odometer reading to the 1/10th mile (0.16 km) at the end of the visibility survey.

Start Time (hhmm): Write in the time to the nearest minute when observers start taking visibility measures, using the hour and minute format shown. Use military time (add 12 to the hour beginning with 1 pm through 11 pm). Fill in all four digits. Examples are 0630 (6:30 am), 0802 (8:02 am). Most sampling will occur during the evenings, therefore you would record 1:30 pm as 1330 and 8:00 pm would be 2000.

End Time (hhmm): Write in the time to the nearest minute when observers stop taking visibility measures, using the hour and minute format shown. Use military time.

GPS File Name (aaaaYYYYdeer#vis): Write in the Park Code (4 digits), year (4 digits), "deer" to identify the project, the survey number (#) 1, 2, or 3, and "vis" to identify this file as containing visibility measures. In most years, the only survey number needed is 1. The GPS File Name recorded on a data sheet must correspond to its associated file name on the GPS unit.

Left Distance (m): On the left side of the vehicle, record the horizontal distance in meters between the observer and a perpendicular point at which they can no longer discern what they are seeing with a spotlight, especially if it is a deer. Use a laser range-finder whenever possible to get as accurate a distance as possible. *Do not round off numbers to the nearest 10 meters (i.e. 70, 80, 90 and so on); estimate the distance to the nearest meter.* Perpendicular measures are taken at each 0.16 km (1/10th mile) stop along the survey route. In areas were visibility is good, such as an open field, record visibility measures out to 250 m but no further.

Right Distance (m): On the right side of the vehicle, record the horizontal distance in meters between the observer and a perpendicular point at which they can no longer discern what they are seeing with a spotlight, as described above for *Left Distance*.

Comments: Record any comments that seem appropriate and that might help someone interpret and analyze the data correctly.

Visibility Estimates for Spotlight Survey
Field Data Form – White-tailed deer spotlight survey data form

Date:___/___/_____ Park:_____ Route:_____ Observers:_____

Beginning Odometer Reading:_____ Ending Odometer Reading:_____

Start Time:_____ End Time:_____ GPS File Name:_____

1/10 mile	Left distance	Right distance	Comment	1/10 mile	Left distance	Right distance	Comment
0.0				3.6			
0.1				3.7			
0.2				3.8			
0.3				3.9			
0.4				4.0			
0.5				4.1			
0.6				4.2			
0.7				4.3			
0.8				4.4			
0.9				4.5			
1.0				4.6			
1.1				4.7			
1.2				4.8			
1.3				4.9			
1.4				5.0			
1.5				5.1			
1.6				5.2			
1.7				5.3			
1.8				5.4			
1.9				5.5			
2.0				5.6			
2.1				5.7			
2.2				5.8			
2.3				5.9			
2.4				6.0			
2.5				6.1			
2.6				6.2			
2.7				6.3			
2.8				6.4			
2.9				6.5			
3.0				6.6			
3.1				6.7			
3.2				6.8			
3.3				6.9			
3.4				7.0			
3.5				7.1			

White-tailed Deer Monitoring Protocol for the Heartland Network Inventory and Monitoring Program

10.7 Standard Operating Procedure 7: Geospatial Data Management

Version 1.00 (August 2007)

Revision History Log:

Prev. Version #	Revision Date	Author	Changes Made	Reason for Change	New Version #

This Standard Operating Procedure (SOP) gives step-by-step instructions on: 1) creating a geodatabase, 2) entering GIS data, 3) working with tables and queries, 4) creating offsets, and 5) creating habitat GIS layers for white-tailed deer surveys on National Park Service lands within the Heartland Network Inventory and Monitoring Program. To complete this SOP, the software Microsoft Access and ArcGIS must be loaded on the computer.

I. Geodatabase Creation

Procedures:

1. Open ArcCatalog and create a new geodatabase.
2. For each UTM (Universal Transverse Mercator) zone that you will be collecting data in, create a feature dataset inside the geodatabase. The name given to the feature dataset should include the UTM zone and the label fds to distinguish it as a feature dataset (Ex. fds_Deer_nad83zone15). Set the coordinate system for the feature dataset. For Heartland Network parks the coordinate system used is UTM NAD83 (Conus) and depending on what park zone 14N – 17N (see SOP #3 page 5 for park zone). Also set the X/Y Domain to the fullest possible extent that data may be collected in.

II. Entering Spatial Data into the Geodatabase

Procedures:

1. Download, differentially correct, and export all Global Positioning System (GPS) rover files from the deer and visibility surveys into shapefiles (see SOP #3).
2. In ArcMap open all the deer location shapefiles for one park for the current year. Use ArcToolbox to merge these files together and save as a single feature class inside the correct feature dataset inside the geodatabase. The new file name should include fcl (to identify it as a feature class), park code, project name, year, and the letter "t" (to identify it as a point layer) (Ex. fclWicrDeerSurveyData2007t).
3. Error check the deer location feature class attribute table fields against the field sheets and clean up any errors.
4. In the attribute table add the field 'DeerID'. This field is a numeric integer. The DeerID field is a unique identification used for all deer observations through all parks and all years. Add this field in ArcMap using the AlaskaPak extension. Highlight the file the field is to be added to. Then select *AlaskaPak*, click on **Add Unique ID**. When the unique ID window opens change *Field Name* to **DeerID**, and in the *Starting Value* type in what the highest DeerID value in the tbl_SurveyData_Master (located in the deer geodatabase) with a 1 added to it.
5. In ArcMap open all the visibility survey location shapefiles for one park for the current year. Use ArcToolbox to merge these files together and save as a single feature class inside the correct feature dataset inside the geodatabase. The new file name should include fcl, park code, Visibility, year, and the letter "t" (to identify it as a point layer) (Ex: fclWicrVisibility2007t).
6. Error check the visibility location feature class attribute table fields against the field sheets and clean up any errors.

III. Geodatabase Tables and Queries

Procedures:

1. First add new deer survey data to the tbl_SurveyData_Master table. This is done by exporting a temporary copy of the new GIS deer locations attribute table (Ex. Copy_fclParkDeerSurveyData20XXt). The temporary table should be saved in the highest level of the geodatabase. Next using an append query (Query1 in geodatabase) add data from **Copy_fclParkDeerSurveyData20XXt** to **tbl_SurveyData_Master**. Once the new data is appended to the master table, delete the temporary table file.
2. The second step is to calculate the perpendicular and parallel distances for the deer location data (see Figure 7.01), which will be used to create the GIS offset layers in section IV. This is done by creating a select query in Microsoft Access. In the query design view add the **tbl_DeerSurvey_Master** table. Next add the following fields to the select query: DeerID, EventID, Replicate, Distance_m, Angle, and Quadrant_C. The final two fields are calculated. The first calculated field will be perpendicular distance and the second will be parallel distance (see Figure 7.02). The equations for

these calculations are below. Once this select query is created it will update automatically each time new data is added to the tbl_DeerSurvey_Master table.

Distance Equations:

y = Sin (u * π/180) * r

x = Cos (u * π/180) * r

u = angle the vehicle is to the deer (Angle field from tbl_SurveyData_Master in database)
r = rangefinder distance (Distance_m field in the tbl_SurveyData_Master in database)
x = parallel distance
y = perpendicular distance
π = pi (3.14159265358979)

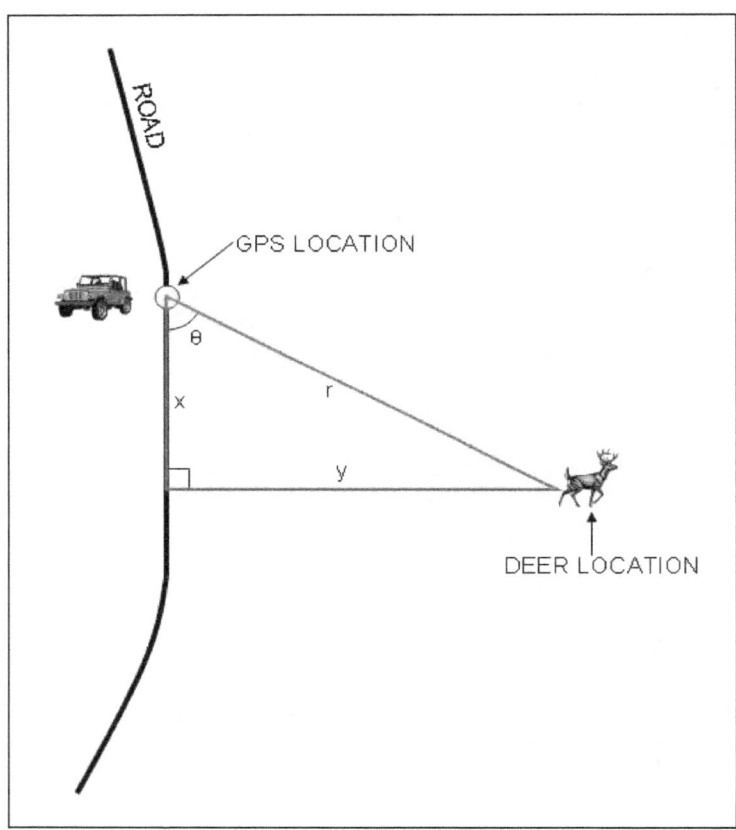

Figure 7.01. Distance equation diagrams.

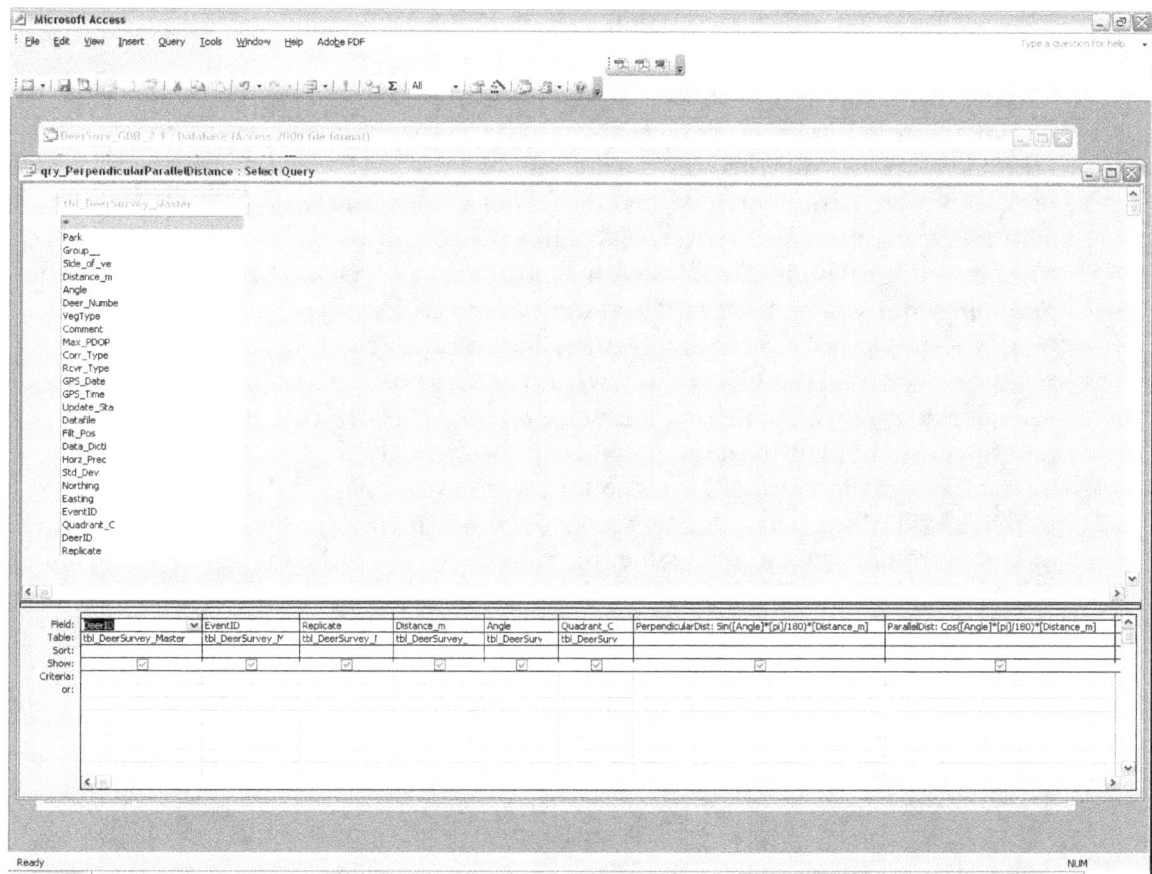

Figure 7.02. Snapshot of the perpendicular and parallel distance select query.

IV. Creation of GIS Offset Layers of Deer Locations

Procedures:

1. *Identify distance tables:* Inside the geodatabase there is a query named **qry_PerpendicularParallelDistance**. This query calculates the perpendicular distance, which is the distance between the deer and the road at a 90 degree angle and the parallel distance, which is the distance along the road between the GPS point on the road and the start of the perpendicular distance. This table will be referenced multiple times in the steps below, so have a copy or a printed version for the park and the year you are working on handy.

2. *Create two new GIS files:* This can be done in ArcCatalog by right mouse clicking, selecting **New,** and then choosing the correct file type. The first file will be a feature class located within the correct feature dataset in the geodatabase. This feature class will become the offset data for the current year. The file name should include fcl (to identify it as a feature class), park code (4 letters), DeerSurveyDataOffset, year, and the letter "t" (to identify it as a point layer). An example is fclWicrDeerSurveyDataOffset2007t. In this file *add* an attribute field called **DeerID.** The second file to create is a temporary line shapefile. This file will be the parallel

distance from the deer location collected with the GPS unit. For the purpose of this document this file will be referred to as LineTemp.shp.

3. Open the program file ArcMap.

4. *Digitize parallel line features:* In the ArcMap project, open the following layers: deer GPS locations on tour road for the current year (ex: fclParkDeerSurveyData20XXt), park tour road, park boundary, and the 2 files created in step 2 (fclParkDeerSurveyDataOffset20XXt and LineTemp).

5. Start the editor with the *Task* as **New Feature** and *Target* as **LineTemp**. Set the *Snapping* tool for the **fclParkDeerSurveyData20XXt** layer only.

6. You will now digitize new line features in the **LineTemp** file using the *sketch tool*. *Click* once on a **fclParkDeerSurveyData20XXt point**. Next input the parallel length measurement for the point you are working on. This can be done by right clicking and selecting Length from the menu or by *typing* **Ctrl^L**. A Length textbox is now open. *Type* in the Parallel Distance for the point and **Enter**. The line is now locked to the length of the parallel distance. Now move the line so that it runs straight out along the road. The directions the line runs depends on the Quadrant_C attribute field for the point, which indicates if the line runs in front or behind the GPS location. When you have the line placed in the correct spot, *double click* the left mouse button to finish the line. Repeat this step for all deer locations.

7. *Digitize deer offsets:* After the LineTemp file is complete, change the editor *Target* to **fclParkDeerSurveyDataOffset20XXt** and the *snapping* options to **fclParkDeerSurveyData20XXt** and **LineTemp**, vertex only for both files.

8. Now digitize the deer offset points (fclParkDeerSurveyDataOffset20XXt) by using the Distance-Distance editor tool. First *click* on the fclParkDeerSurveyData20XXt point. Next *type* **D** on the keyboard, this opens a distance textbox. *Type* in the value **Distance_m** from the table and **Enter**. You will see a circular buffer appear around the point. Then *click* on the far end of the LineTemp line and *type* **D** on the keyboard again, *type* the **perpendicular distance** in and **Enter**. Notice that your mouse snaps to the locations that the two circles intersect. See what your Quadrant_C attribute says (right or left) and *click* on the intersecting point on the correct side. *Attribute* the table with the correct DeerID number. Repeat this step for all deer locations.

9. Make sure all edits are saved and *click* **Stop Editing** from the Editor menu.

V. Creation of GIS Habitat Layers

Procedures:

1. In ArcCatalog create two new files. The first file will be a feature class polygon saved in the correct feature dataset in the geodatabase. This file will be the visibility extent that can be seen during the deer surveys. Name the file fcl, park code, DeerHabitat, year, and the letter "p" (to identify it as a polygon layer) (Ex: fclWicrDeerHabitat2007p). The second file will be a temporary line shapefile. This file can be named anything as long as you remember what the name is until the completion of this section. For the purposes of this document the file will be called VisTemp.shp.

2. Open ArcMap and *add* the following layers to the project: fclParkDeerHabitat20XXp, VisTemp, tour road, park boundary, and fclParkVisibility20XXt.

3. In this step, if more then one night of visibility estimates are made it helps to either display only one night of visibility points out of the number taken (by using the definition query) or display the different nights in different colors or symbols. Open the attribute table for the visibility points. Start the Editor, select **New Feature** as the *Task* and **VisTemp** as the *Target*. The *snapping* tool should be set for the **fclParkVisibility20XXt** file. You will now digitize the rangefinders lines of sight. *Click* on the first visibility point and then *press* **Ctrl^L** on the keyboard (this brings up the length textbox). *Type* in Left Side of the Vehicle measurement and **Enter**. Move your line so that it is on the left side of the road at a perpendicular angle to the road. Next *click* on the same visibility point and then *press* **Ctrl^L** on the keyboard (this brings up the length textbox). *Type* in Right Side of the Vehicle measurement and **Enter**. Move your line so that it is on the right side of the road at a perpendicular angle to the road. Do this for all visibility GPS points.

4. Once all VisTemp lines are created, the next step is to digitize the habitat polygon. In the ArcMap project open the deer offset layer for the park and year you are working on. Then on the Editor toolbar change the *target* to **fclParkDeerHabitat20XXp** and the *snapping* to **VisTemp** vertex only and **fclParkDeerSurveyDataOffset20XXt**. Next digitize the habitat polygon. Start with the first VisTemp line on the left of the road and *click* on the end of the line. Now digitize the polygon along the outside edges of the VisTemp layer and if the fclParkDeerSurveyDataOffset20XXt layer is beyond the VisTemp digitize it into the habitat polygon (see Figure 7.03). When finished digitizing *click* **Save** and **Stop** editing.

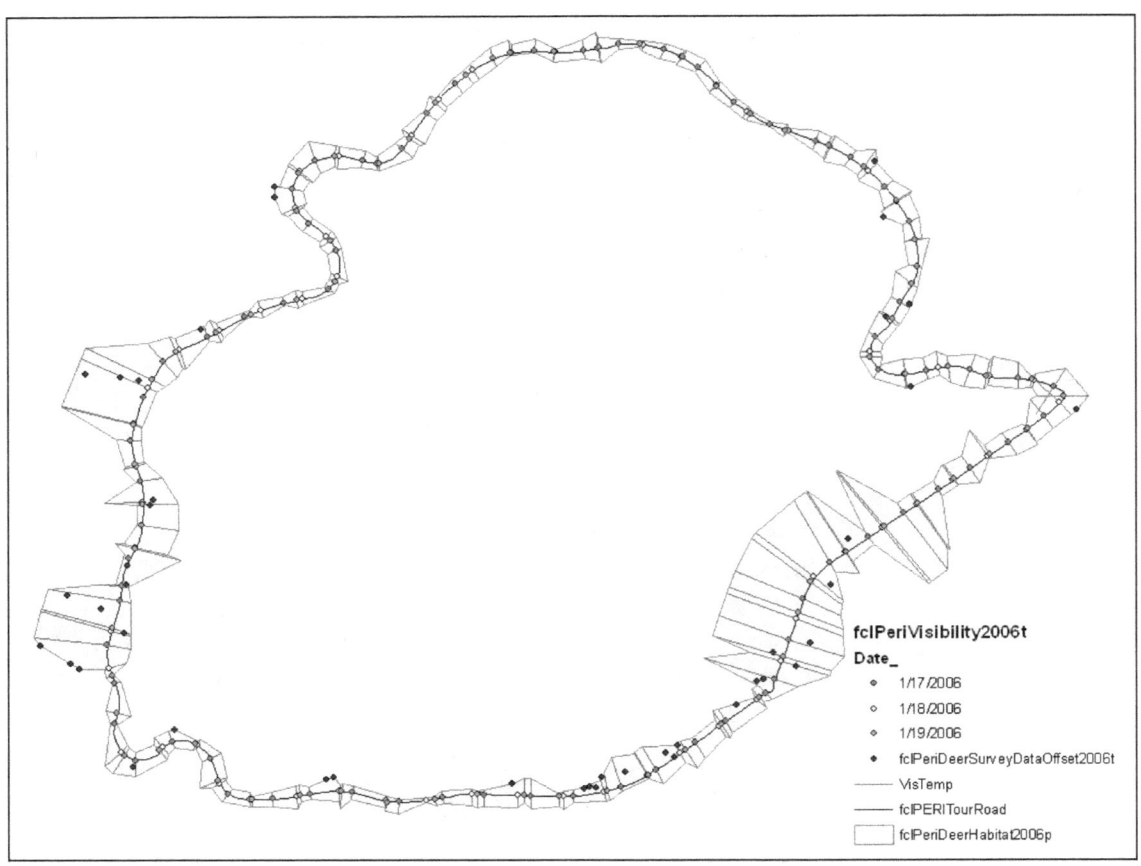

Figure 7.03. Example of deer visibility and habitat GIS layers.

5. Finally add the acreage measurement to fclParkDeerHabitat20XXp file. This can be done by highlighting the file in the ArcMap data view and *selecting* **Add Acres/Miles** from the AlaskaPak extension menu. The completed geodatabase should resemble Figure 7.04.

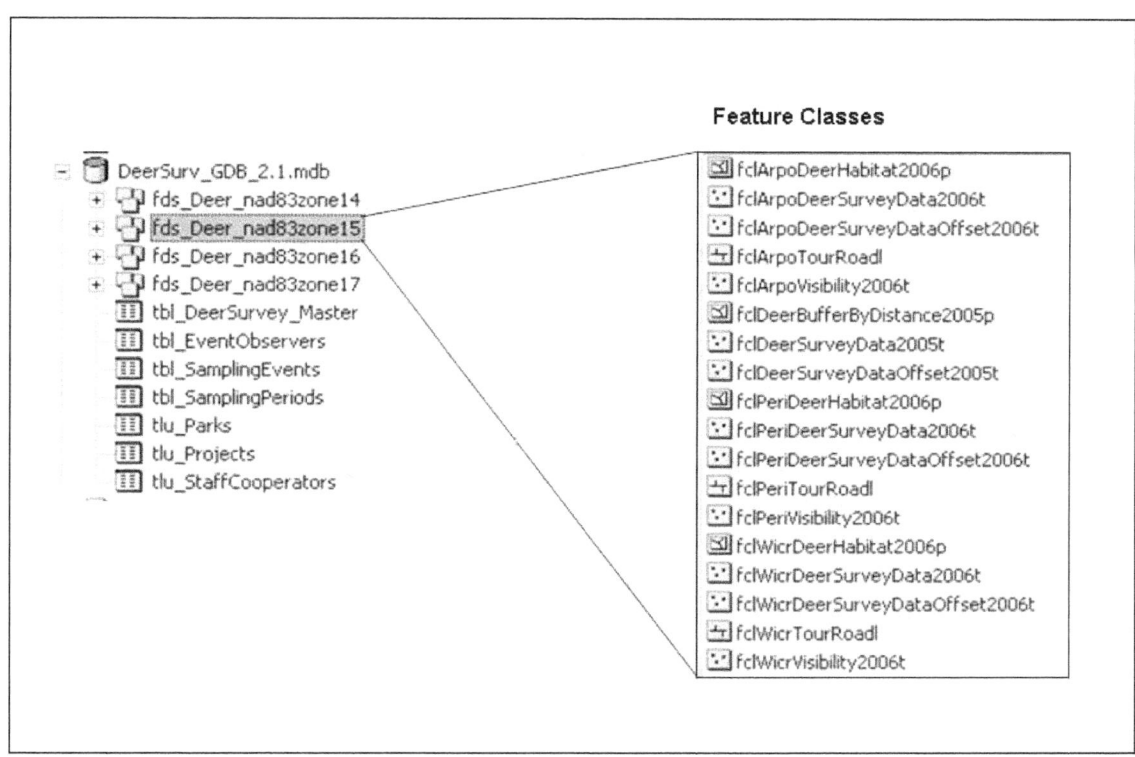

Figure 7.04. File tree of the deer geodatabase.

White-tailed Deer Monitoring Protocol for the Heartland Network Inventory and Monitoring Program

10.8 Standard Operating Procedure 8: Data Management

Version 1.00 (August 2007)

Revision History Log:

Prev. Version #	Revision Date	Author	Changes Made	Reason for Change	New Version #

This Standard Operating Procedure (SOP) gives step-by-step instructions on how to manage data for white-tailed deer monitoring on National Park Service lands within the Heartland Network Inventory and Monitoring Program.

I. Metadata

Data for the white-tailed deer monitoring project is maintained in an ArcGIS (ESRI, Inc.) geodatabase called Deer_Surv_GDB. Use of a geodatabase allows the data manager to take advantage of the ArcGIS metadata utilities. The geodatabase itself is simply a container for the data. Metadata specifically addresses *feature datasets* and the *feature classes* which are contained in the geodatabase.

Detailed metadata including attribute information should be created for each feature class.

Procedure:

1. Open ArcCatalog.
2. Highlight DeerSurv_GDB_2.1 from the directory in the left window.
3. Select FGDC ESRI in the Stylesheet on the upper left part of the window.
4. Expand the directory tree so that the geodatabase is expanded to show all of the feature datasets and feature classes.
5. Highlight a feature class in the left window.
6. In the right window, there are three tabs: Contents", "Preview" and "Metadata".
7. Click on the "Metadata" tab.
8. If metadata has already been created, there will be entries for "Description", "Spatial" and "Attributes" sections.

60

9. Preview the existing metadata by clicking on the various tabs and headings.
10. To edit the existing metadata, click on the button (pencil and paper icon) to the right of the Stylesheet combo box.
11. A form will appear for editing the metadata (see Figure 8.01).
12. Fill out the form and save your changes.
13. Export the new or modified metadata.
14. Click on the export button to the right of the Style Sheet selection on the top bar.
15. Save in XML format as this is the industry standard for metadata. Do not use html format except for display purposes.
16. Upload metadata (XML file) to the WASO clearinghouse, NR-GIS or the equivalent. Contact WASO I&M staff for the latest upload procedures (see Section V below for current procedures).

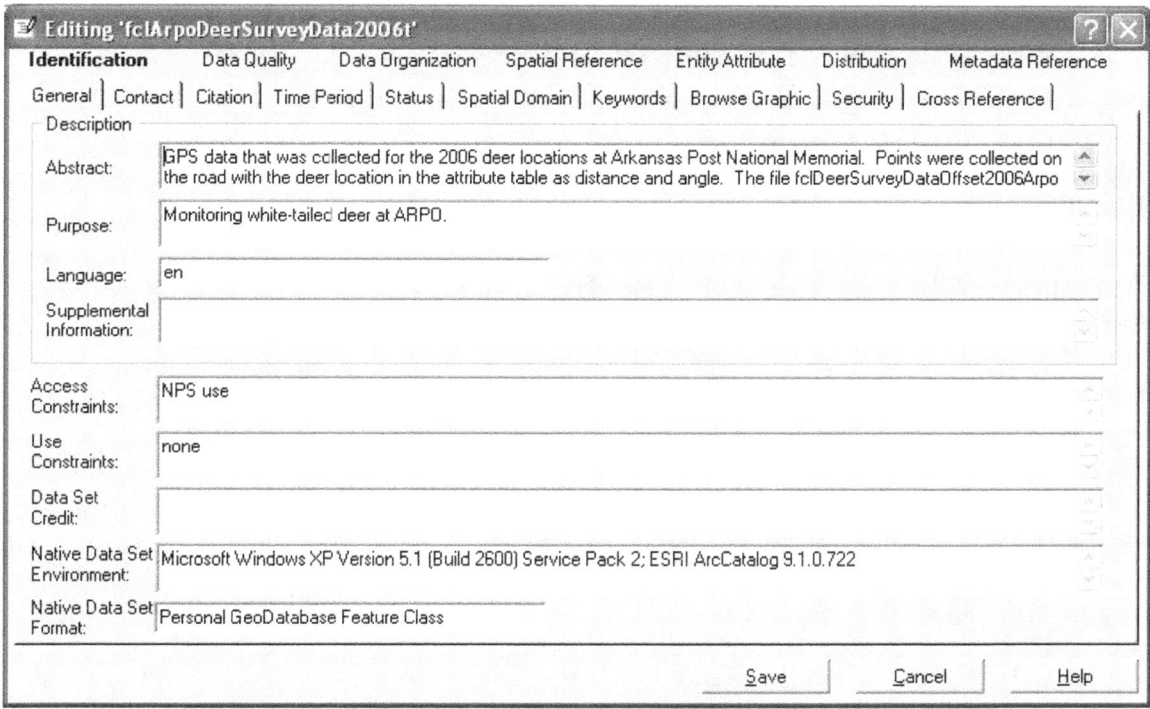

Figure 8.01 – Metadata editing tool for ArcGIS feature classes.

II. Data Model

The data model for the deer monitoring geodatabase is shown in Figure 8.02 below. The geodatabase should be maintained in three parts: (a) event-related data such as weather and start/end times for each survey; (b) deer observations and locations logged into the GPS using a data dictionary and (c) purely spatial data gathered by the GPS unit. Both (b) and (c) should be directly imported from the GPS into the GIS.

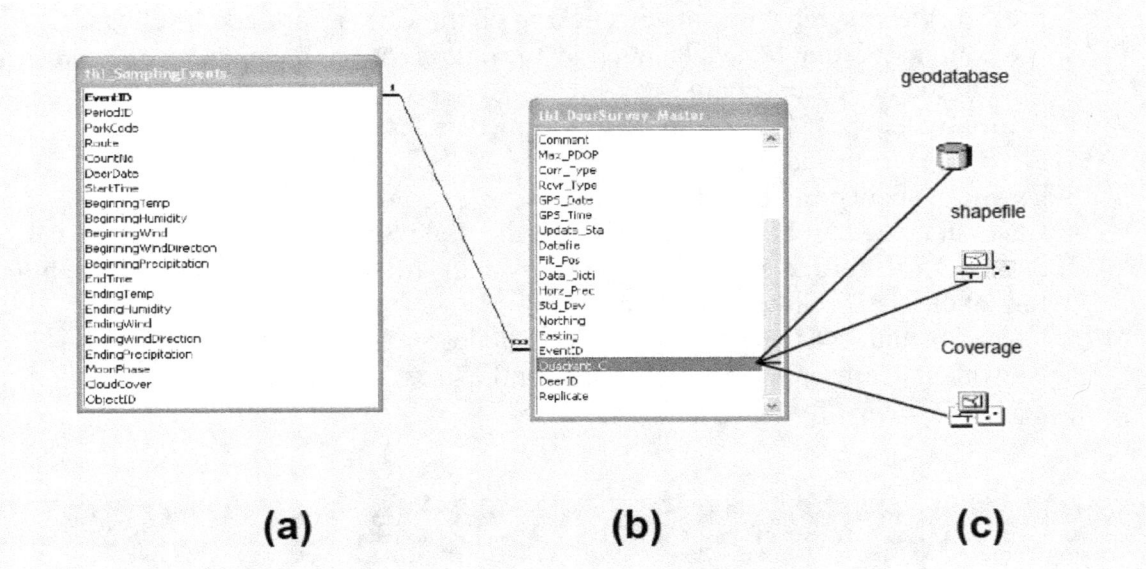

Figure 8.02 – Entity relationship diagram for Deer_Surv_GDB_2.1

III. Data Entry

Data entry is limited to event-related data. This data is recorded at the top of each spotlight survey form. The data must be entered manually into Access.

Procedure:

1. Open the geodatabase using Access.
2. The Event data form will appear (see Figure 8.03 below).
3. Select the PeriodID for the sampling event.
4. New periodIDs should be created by the project leader by filling out a new record in tbl_SamplingPeriods. The new periodID will appear on the SamplingEvents form.
5. Enter the date, start time, end time, name of the route and count #. Count # will usually be one because most surveys pass only once on the survey route. If more than one survey is conducted, then increment the count #.
6. Enter observer initials.
7. Make entries at the start and end of the survey for: temperature, humidity, wind speed, wind direction and precipitation.
8. Complete one record for each survey.

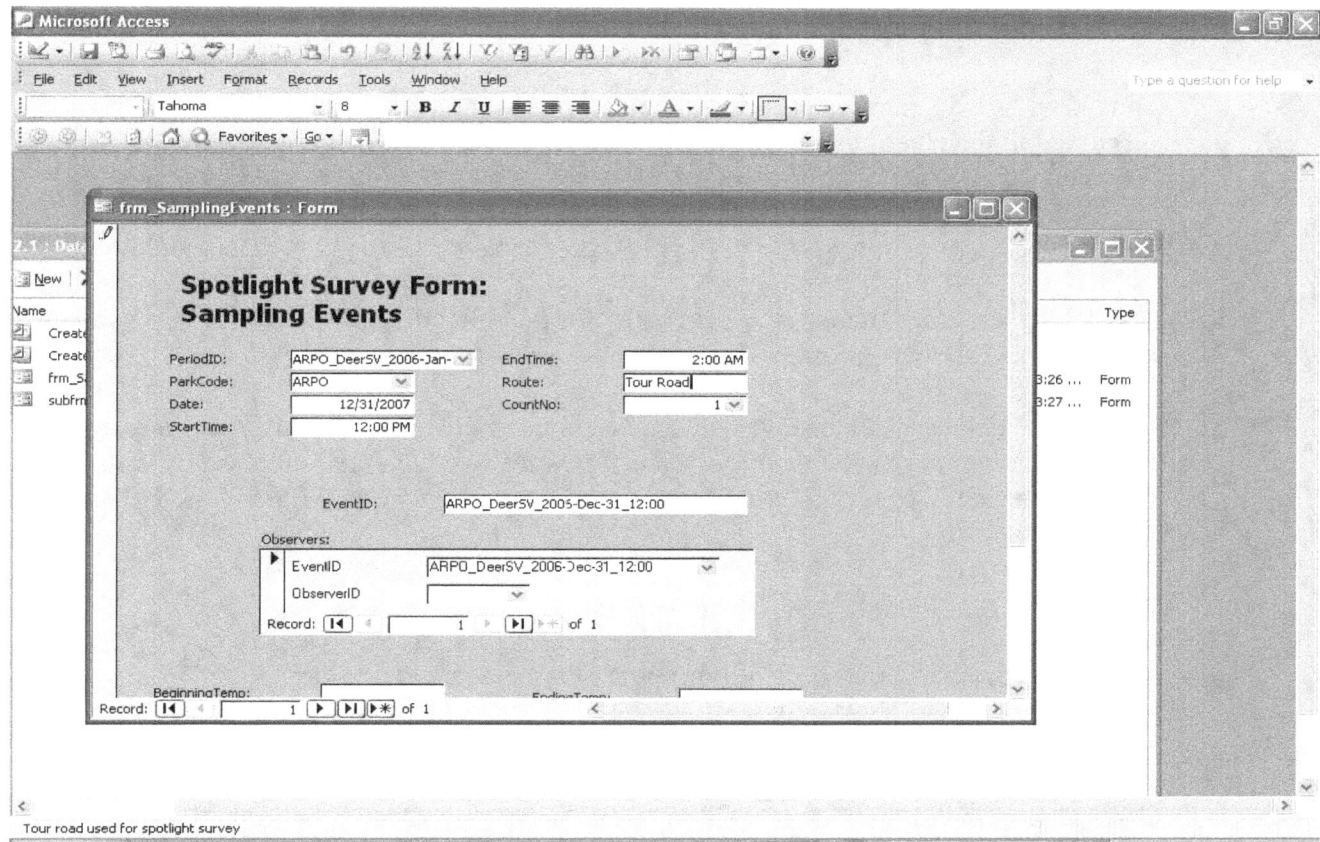

Figure 8.03 – Data entry form for Sampling Event records.

IV. Data Verification and Validation

Data verification and validation is greatly simplified by using a detailed data dictionary with the GPS unit. Field data entry for deer counts represents most of the monitoring data. Since it is already in electronic format, copy errors from paper data sheets to the database are eliminated. Data verification of weather data is still necessary. Follow the directions below for both tbl_SamplingEvents and tbl_EventObservers.

Procedure:

1. Open the table.
2. Print records corresponding to the current year.
3. Verify all values with original field data sheets.
4. Make corrections directly to the table.
5. Repeat steps 3 and 4 until there are no errors.

Data validation for deer counts is accomplished through the geodatabase. EventID related data is validated entirely through the data entry form. PeriodIDs are restricted to table-based pick lists; park and EventIDs are auto-generated by PeriodID, date and time. Weather and physical conditions are limited by control validation rules, that is, range limits for values entered into text fields.

63

V. Database Administration and Availability

Details on how to administer monitoring databases and how to make them available are discussed in the Heartland Network Data Management Plan. The Plan may be downloaded at:

http://www1.nature.nps.gov/im/units/htln/data_management/data_management.htm

Availability of metadata is critical. In order for potential data users to know the available data products at your program, they must have access to metadata.

Posting the databases themselves on clearinghouse websites is less critical. They are dynamic and quickly become out-of-date. They are also large and more easily distributed on an "as needed" basis via "ftp". Metadata may be uploaded to NPS WASO NR-GIS clearinghouse at

http://science.nature.nps.gov/nrdata/

Detailed procedures are provided for uploading metadata at this site.

VI. References

Rowell, Gareth A., Michael H. Williams and Michael D. DeBacker. 2005. Data Management Plan: Heartland I&M Network And Prairie Cluster Prototype Monitoring Program.

White-tailed Deer Monitoring Protocol for the Heartland Network Inventory and Monitoring Program

10.9 Standard Operating Procedure 9: Data Summary and Analysis

Version 1.00 (August 2007)

Revision History Log:

Prev. Version #	Revision Date	Author	Changes Made	Reason for Change	New Version #

This Standard Operating Procedure (SOP) gives step-by-step instructions on how to summarize and analyze white-tailed deer monitoring data collected on National Park Service lands within the Heartland Network Inventory and Monitoring Program. A critical component of any long-term monitoring protocol is a consistent and systematic way of analyzing and reporting on information (data) collected. The information must serve two purposes: (1) describe the current condition or status of a deer population, and (2) detect changes in a population through time.

I. Data Summary

Index of Relative Abundance

The variable selected for data summary purposes is an index of relative population density. This index is positively related to absolute abundance, but to an unknown degree. This annual index of relative population density provides information to park managers on trends in park deer populations and may provide feedback on the effects of implemented management efforts (e.g., population control or vegetation restoration efforts). This index of relative population density, defined as the number of individuals observed from the road/km^2, allows evaluation of annual change in addition to long-term trends. To calculate this index of relative abundance, two pieces of information are needed: (1) the number of individuals within the sample area, and (2) the size of the area sampled.

Procedures:

1. Using the area surveyed annually (see SOP #7 "Geospatial Data Management" for details on determining annual survey areas), calculate the index of nightly deer densities for a park as:

$$D = C / A$$

> D = index of deer density in individuals/km^2
> C = maximum number of deer counted
> A = annual area surveyed (km^2)

2. Calculate the annual mean deer density and standard deviation from the nightly maximum deer counts for that year, usually six.
3. Determine the range in deer population densities each year from replicate values.

Mapping Deer Distribution

The locations of individual deer and deer groups will be mapped for the monitoring period (Figure 9.01). Areas where deer congregate in the park and preferred habitats are easily visualized from the map. All deer maps are to be created by using ArcGIS. The layout of the maps should have a similar look to them from year to year and park to park.

Procedure:

1. Open ArcMap
2. Add the following layers to the map dataview: deer locations, park boundary, and the most current park image for the background.
3. On the map layout add the following items: scale bar in meters, scale text, legend, and north arrow.
4. When finished export the map as a .jpeg and store in the project folder.

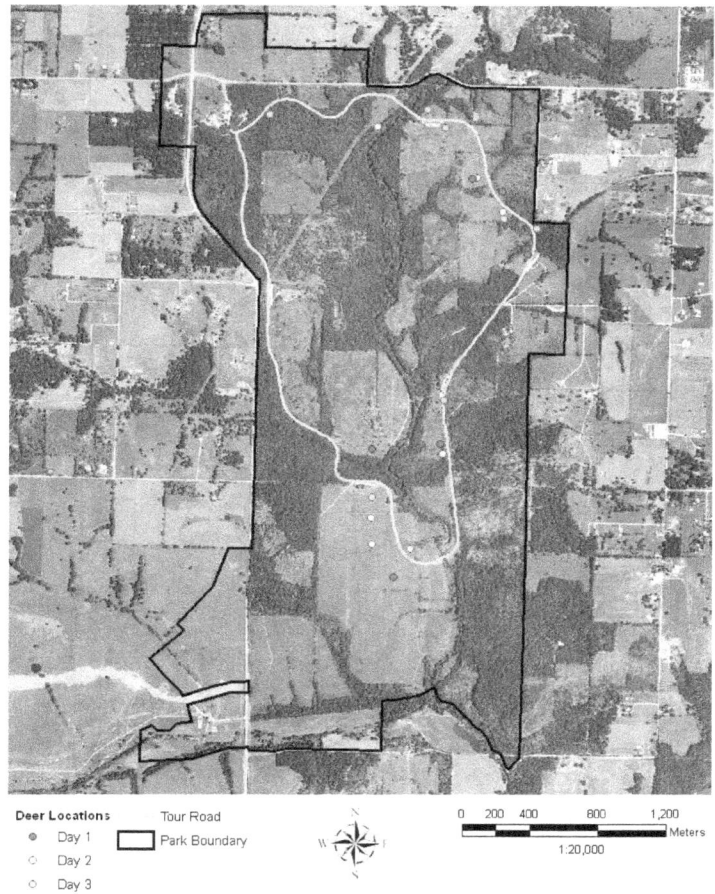

Figure 9.01 - Distribution of deer at Wilson's Creek National Battlefield, 2006.

II. Data Analysis

<u>Recommendations for Routine Data Summaries and Analyses</u>

Procedures:

1. The percent change in annual deer densities from the previous year is calculated as follows:

$$\pm\% \text{ change} = [(\text{second year density} - \text{first year density}) / \text{first year density}] \times 100$$

<u>Recommendations for Long-term Trend Analyses</u>

Procedures:

1. The primary method of evaluating long-term trends will be to plot point estimates of relative abundance, along with some associated measure of variability or reliability over time. Graphs are easily interpretable and serve as useful tools for interpreting

monitoring results by resource managers. Standard deviations or standard errors serve as estimates of variability; confidence limits serve as estimates of reliability.

Confidence limits are expressed in terms of a confidence coefficient. Although the choice of confidence coefficient is somewhat arbitrary, in practice 90% and 95% are the most commonly used.

Confidence limits $(1 - \square)$ are defined as (assuming a normal distribution):

$$Y \pm t_{(\square/2, N-1)} \, s / \sqrt{N}$$

where Y is the sample mean, s is the sample standard deviation, N is the sample size, $\square$ is the desired significance level, and $t_{(\square/2, N-1)}$ is the upper critical value of the t distribution with N - 1 degrees of freedom.

White-tailed Deer Monitoring Protocol for the Heartland Network Inventory and Monitoring Program

10.10 Standard Operating Procedure 10: Reporting

Version 1.00 (August 2007)

Revision History Log:

Prev. Version #	Revision Date	Author	Changes Made	Reason for Change	New Version #

I. Report Format

Template

The report template for Natural Resource Technical Reports should be followed (http://www.nature.nps.gov/publications/NRPM/index.cfm). Natural resource reports are the designated medium for disseminating high priority, current natural resource management information with managerial application. The Natural Resource Technical Reports series is used to disseminate the peer-reviewed results of scientific studies in the physical, biological, and social sciences for both the advancement of science and the achievement of the National Park Service's mission.

Style

Standards for scientific writing as recommended in the CBE Style Manual (CBE Style Manual Committee 1994) should be followed. Reports should be direct and concise. Refer also to Mack (1986), Goldwasser (1999), Day and Gastel (2006), and Strunk and White (2000) for guidelines on appropriate writing style.

Types of Reports and Review Process

Table 10.1 summarizes the types of reports produced and review process. Adapted from DeBacker *et al.* 2005.

Type of Report	Purpose of Report	Primary Audience	Review Process	Frequency
Annual Status Reports for Specific Protocols	Summarize monitoring data collected during the year and provide an update on the status of selected natural resources. Document related data management activities and data summaries.	Park resource managers and external scientists	Internal peer review by HTLN staff	Annually
Executive Summary of Annual Reports for Specific Protocols	Same as Annual Status Reports but summarized to highlight key points for non-technical audiences.	Superintendents, interpreters, and the general public	Internal peer review by HTLN staff	Simultaneous with Annual Status Reports
Comprehensive Trends and Analysis and Synthesis Reports	Describe and interpret trends in individual vital signs. Describe and interpret relationships among observed trends and park management, known stressors, climate, *etc*. Highlight resources of concern that may require management action.	Park resource managers and external scientists	Internal peer review by HTLN staff	Every 5-7 years
Executive Summary of Comprehensive Trends and Analysis and Synthesis Reports	Same as Comprehensive Trends and Analysis and Synthesis Reports, but summarized to highlight findings and recommendations for non-technical audiences.	Superintendents, interpreters, and the general public	Internal peer review by HTLN staff	Simultaneous with Comprehensive Trends Analysis and Synthesis Reports

Report Distribution

Following review, annual reports will be distributed by September 1st of the year in which data is collected. Reports can also be distributed to partners involved in conservation of the monitored resource. This determination is made by the park, the network, or the regional office. All data collected is public property and subject to requests under the Freedom of Information Act (FOIA). However, sensitive data, such as the location of rare species, must be withheld in some cases. Reports containing non-sensitive data will be made publicly available and disseminated through the network website.

IV. References

CBE Style Manual Committee. 1994. Scientific style and format: the CBE manual for authors, editors, and publishers. 6th edition. Council of Biology Editors, Cambridge University Press, New York, New York.

Day, R. A. and B. Gastel. 2006. How to write and publish a scientific paper. 6th edition. Greenwood Press, Westport, CT.

DeBacker, M. D., C. C. Young, P. Adams., L. Morrison, D. Peitz, G. A. Rowell, M. Williams, and D. Bowles. 2005. Heartland Inventory and Monitoring and Prairie Cluster Prototype Monitoring Program vital signs monitoring plan. U.S. National Park Service, Heartland I&M Network and Prairie Cluster Prototype Monitoring Program, Wilson's Creek National Battlefield, Republic, Missouri.

Goldwasser, L. 1999. A collection of grammatical points. Bulletin of the Ecological Society of America. **79**: 148-150.

Mack, R. N. 1986. Writing with precision, clarity, and economy. Bulletin of Ecological Society of America **67**:31-35.

Strunk, W., Jr., and E. B. White. 2000. The Elements of Style. 4th Edition. Macmillan, New York, New York.

White-tailed Deer Monitoring Protocol for the Heartland Network Inventory and Monitoring Program

10.11 Standard Operating Procedure 11: Procedures and Equipment Storage after the Field Season

Version 1.00 (August 2007)

Revision History Log:

Prev. Version #	Revision Date	Author	Changes Made	Reason for Change	New Version #

This Standard Operating Procedure (SOP) gives step-by-step instructions that all field observers using the white-tailed deer survey protocol should be familiar with and follow after the field season is completed.

Procedures:

1. Clean and repair all equipment prior to returning it to the proper storage areas in the HTLN storage building, office, or mobile trailer. All reference materials and extra data sheets should be filed in their appropriate filing cabinet. Clean the insides and outsides of all vehicles used in the field.

2. Organize field data sheets and check that they have been filled out completely. As a rule, all data sheets should be reviewed for completeness before the crew leaves the field. However, because of the number of field days and crew members, some deficiencies in data recording may not be identified until all data sheet have been organized and reviewed as a group. If this situation arises, all attempts to locate deficient information should be made. If this is not possible, then an explanation on what information is missing should be placed in the trip report for that sampling event. Trip reports are links to their corresponding data through the database.

3. Identify and obtain ancillary data. It is of critical importance that this data be incorporated into the deer monitoring efforts. First and foremost, knowledge of management efforts in a park for that year will be used to assess the effects of these efforts on deer numbers present. Certain plants affected by a management action may be utilized for food, cover, or bedding habitat by deer, thus altering the number of deer observed. Climate can also influence deer numbers, both directly and indirectly. Therefore, annual climate data will be obtained from active weather stations in or near each park.

4. At the end of each field trip, file a trip report with the data manager, outlining daily accomplishments, hours worked, field-crew members and their responsibilities, and

any unique situations encountered. This information is incorporated in the database and used during data analysis. This information is critical for identifying causes of discrepancies and inconsistencies in the data. The project manager is responsible for filing all trip reports.

White-tailed Deer Monitoring Protocol for the Heartland Network Inventory and Monitoring Program

Version 1.00 (August 2007)

Revision History Log:

Prev. Version #	Revision Date	Author	Changes Made	Reason for Change	New Version #

This Standard Operating Procedure (SOP) explains how to make changes to the white-tailed deer monitoring Protocol Narrative and accompanying SOPs, and tracking these changes. Observers asked to edit the Protocol Narrative or any one of the SOPs need to follow this outlined procedure in order to eliminate confusion in how data is collected and analyzed. All observers should be familiar with this SOP in order to identify and use the most current methodologies.

Procedures:

1. The narrative for the "White-tailed Deer Monitoring Protocol for the Heartland Network Inventory and Monitoring Program" and accompanying SOPs has attempted to incorporate the most sound, up-to-date methodologies for collecting and analyzing deer data. However, all protocols regardless of how sound require editing as new and different information becomes available. Required edits should be made in a timely manner and appropriate reviews undertaken.
2. All edits require review for clarity and technical soundness. Small changes or additions to existing methods will be reviewed in-house by HTLN staff. However, if a complete change in methods is sought, an outside review is required. Regional and national staff of the National Park Service with familiarity in deer monitoring and data analysis will be utilized as reviewers. Experts in deer research and statistical methodologies outside of the National Park Service will be utilized in the review process as well.
3. Document edits and protocol versioning in the Revision History Log that accompanies the Protocol Narrative and each SOP. Log changes in the Protocol Narrative or SOP being edited only. Version numbers increase incrementally by hundredths (e.g., version 1.01, version 1.02, ...etc.) for minor changes. Major revisions should be designated with the next whole number (e.g., version 2.00, 3.00, 4.00 ...). Record the previous version number, date of revision, author of the revision, identify paragraphs and pages where changes are made, and the reason for making the changes along with the new version number.
4. Inform the Data Manager about changes to the Protocol Narrative or SOP so the new version number can be incorporated in the Metadata of the project database. The database may have to be edited by the Data Manager to accompany changes in the Protocol Narrative and SOPs.

5. Post new versions on the internet and forward copies to all individuals with a previous version of the affected Protocol Narrative or SOP.

The NPS has organized its parks with significant natural resources into 32 networks linked by geography and shared natural resource characteristics. HTLN is composed of 15 National Park Service (NPS) units in eight Midwestern states. These parks contain a wide variety of natural and cultural resources including sites focused on commemorating civil war battlefields, Native American heritage, westward expansion, and our U.S. Presidents. The Network is charged with creating inventories of its species and natural features as well as monitoring trends and issues in order to make sound management decisions. Critical inventories help park managers understand the natural resources in their care while monitoring programs help them understand meaningful change in natural systems and to respond accordingly. The Heartland Network helps to link natural and cultural resources by protecting the habitat of our history.

The I&M program bridges the gap between science and management with a third of its efforts aimed at making information accessible. Each network of parks, such as Heartland, has its own multi-disciplinary team of scientists, support personnel, and seasonal field technicians whose system of online databases and reports make information and research results available to all. Greater efficiency is achieved through shared staff and funding as these core groups of professionals augment work done by individual park staff. Through this type of integration and partnership, network parks are able to accomplish more than a single park could on its own.

The mission of the Heartland Network is to collaboratively develop and conduct scientifically credible inventories and long-term monitoring of park "vital signs" and to distribute this information for use by park staff, partners, and the public, thus enhancing understanding which leads to sound decision making in the preservation of natural resources and cultural history held in trust by the National Park Service.

www.nature.nps.gov/im/units/htln/

Natural Resource Monitoring

The Department of the Interior protects and manages the nation's natural resources and cultural heritage; provides scientific and other information about those resources; and honors its special responsibilities to American Indians, Alaska Natives, and affiliated Island Communities.

NPS D-70, August 2007